Meeting Skills for Leaders

Make meetings more productive

Fourth Edition

Marion E. Haynes

Viva Books
New Delhi | Mumbai | Chennai | Kolkata
Bengaluru | Hyderabad | Kochi | Guwahati

First Indian Edition 2011

VIVA BOOKS PRIVATE LIMITED

- 4737/23 Ansari Road, Daryaganj, New Delhi 110 002
  E-mail: vivadelhi@vivagroupindia.net, Tel. 42242200
- 76, Service Industries, Shirvane, Sector 1, Nerul, Navi Mumbai 400 706
  E-mail: vivamumbai@vivagroupindia.net, Tel. 27721273, 27721274
- Jamals Fazal Chambers, 26 Greams Road, Chennai 600 006
  E-mail: vivachennai@vivagroupindia.net, Tel. 28290304, 28294241
- B-103, Jindal Towers, 21/1A/3 Darga Road, Kolkata 700 017
  E-mail: vivakolkata@vivagroupindia.net, Tel. 22836381, 22816713
- 7, Sovereign Park Apartments, 56-58, K. R. Road, Basavanagudi, Bengaluru 560 004
  E-mail: vivabangalore@vivagroupindia.net, Tel. 26607409, 26607410
- 101-102 Mughal Marc Aptt., 3-4-637 to 641, Narayanguda, Hyderabad 500 029
  E-mail: vivahyderabad@vivagroupindia.net, Tel. 27564481, 27564482
- First Floor, Beevi Towers, SRM Road, Kaloor, Kochi 682 018, Kerala
  E-mail: vivakochi@vivagroupindia.net, Tel: 0484-2403055, 2403056
- 232, GNB Road, Beside UCO Bank, Silpukhuri, Guwahati 781 003
  E-mail: vivaguwahati@vivagroupindia.net, Tel: 0361-2666386

www.vivagroupindia.com

Published by arrangement with

Axzo Press, LLC
562, Willow Brook Office Park
Fairport, New York 14450

ISBN : 978-81-309-1834-1

Published by Vinod Vasishtha for Viva Books Private Limited, 4737/23, Ansari Road, Daryaganj, New Delhi - 110 002. Printed and bound by Raj Press, R-3, Inderpuri, New Delhi - 110 012.

Table of Contents

About the Author

Marion E. Haynes is the author of three titles in the Crisp 50-Minute Series. He has published 35 articles and 10 books on management and supervisory practices, as well as on retirement and life planning.

Mr. Haynes is a graduate of Arizona State University with a BS degree in Business Administration. He holds the MBA degree, with distinction, from New York University.

He retired from Shell Oil Company in 1991 after a 35-year career in human resource management. At retirement, he was the corporate-level manager of pensioner relations. Following retirement, he joined the staff of Price-Waterhouse as a consultant. He worked as a member of a three-person team presenting retirement planning workshops for Price-Waterhouse clients.

Mr. Haynes was appointed an adjunct professor at the University of Houston's College of Continuing Education. He also served as an instructor for the hospitality industry's executive course, presented each year by the university's Conrad Hilton College of Hotel and Restaurant Management, and presented public workshops at several universities in the south-central U.S.

He served for four years on the board of directors of Sheltering Arms, a social services agency for the elderly in Houston, Texas. During this time, he chaired the agency's personnel committee and served on its executive committee.

He was a member of the board of directors of the International Society for Retirement Planning for eight years, serving as president from 1991 to 1993. He also chaired the editorial board for the society's journal and served on its newsletter board.

Today he and his wife, Janice, live in Kerrville, Texas, where he pursues his interests in writing, community service, and travel.

Learning Objectives

Complete this book, and you'll know how to:

1) Select the right type of meeting to hold, and plan it effectively.
2) Select and arrange facilities and equipment best suited to each situation.
3) Conduct meetings that are interactive and productive.
4) Lead stimulating discussions and handle conflict effectively.
5) Evaluate meeting effectiveness and take steps to improve future meetings.

Workplace and Management Competencies mapping

For over 30 years, business and industry has utilized competency models to select employees. The trend to use competency-based approaches in education and training, assessment, and development of workers has experienced a more recent emergence within the Employment and Training Administration (ETA), a division of the United States Department of Labor.

The ETA's General Competency Model Framework spans a wide array of competencies from the more basic competencies, such as reading and writing, to more advanced occupation-specific competencies. The Viva-Crisp Series finds its home in what the ETA refers to as the Workplace Competencies and the Management Competencies.

Meeting Skills for Leaders covers information vital to mastering the following competencies:

Workplace Competencies:

- Problem Solving & Decision Making
- Scheduling & Coordinating

Management Competencies:

- Supporting Others
- Managing Conflict & Team Building

About the Viva-Crisp 50-Minute Series

The Viva-Crisp 50-Minute Series was designed to cover critical business and professional development topics in the shortest possible time. Our easy-to-read, easy-to-understand format can be used for self-study or for classroom training. With a wealth of hands-on exercises, the 50-Minute books keep you engaged and help you retain critical skills.

What You Need to Know

We designed the Viva-Crisp 50-Minute Series to be as self-explanatory as possible. But there are a few things you should know before you begin the book.

Exercises

Exercises look like this:

EXERCISE TITLE

Questions and other information would be here.

Keep a pencil handy. Any time you see an exercise, you should try to complete it. If the exercise has specific answers, an answer key will be provided in the appendix. (Some exercises ask you to think about your own opinions or situation; these types of exercises will not have answer keys.)

Forms

A heading like this means that the rest of the page is a form:

FORMHEAD

Forms are meant to be reusable. You might want to make a photocopy of a form before you fill it out, so that you can use it again later.

A Note to Instructors

We've tried to make the Viva-Crisp 50-Minute Series books as useful as possible as classroom training manuals. Here are some of the features we provide for instructors:

- PowerPoint presentations
- Answer keys
- Assessments
- Customization

PowerPoint Presentations

You can download a PowerPoint presentation for this book from our Web site at www.CrispSeries.com.

Answer keys

If an exercise has specific answers, an answer key will be provided in the appendix. (Some exercises ask you to think about your own opinions or situation; these types of exercises will not have answer keys.)

Assessments

For each 50-Minute Series book, we have developed a 35- to 50-item assessment. The assessment for this book is available at www.CrispSeries.com. *Assessments should not be used in any employee-selection process.*

PART 1

The Effective Meeting

> *A star shone at the hour of our meeting."*
>
> **–J.R.R. Tolkien**

In this part:

- Defining an Effective Meeting
- Planning an Effective Meeting
- Face-to-Face or Virtual?
- Developing an Agenda
- Selecting Participants
- Notifying Participants
- Choosing a Meeting Time
- Dealing with Common Meeting Problems

Defining an Effective Meeting

A meeting is a gathering of three or more people sharing common objectives, where communication (oral and/or written) is the primary means of achieving those objectives.

A meeting is effective when:

- It achieves its objectives.
- It takes a minimum amount of time.
- Participants are satisfied in relation to the time and the objectives.

Problems with Meetings

Many people who regularly participate in meetings report that a majority of the meetings are ineffective. For example, one survey[1] of 635 executives found that 75% of them were "bothered" by the ineffectiveness of typical meetings they attend.

Write down three things that bother you about meetings you attend.

1. ____
2. ____
3. ____

Compare your reaction to the meetings you attend to the following negative meeting characteristics listed in the executive survey:

Meeting Characteristic	"Bothered a Lot"
Drifting off subject	83%
Poor preparation	77%
Questionable effectiveness	74%
Lack of listening	68%
Verbosity of participants	62%
Length	60%
Lack of participation	51%

[1] Reprinted with permission from the American Society for Training and Development, from *Training and Development*, "Achieving Effective Meetings—Not Easy But Possible," by Bradford D. Smart. © 1974, American Society for Training and Development. All rights reserved.

EVALUATE A MEETING

Consider the meetings you typically attend. Compare them to the following characteristics. Place a check (✓) beside statements that apply to your meetings:

____ 1. An agenda is prepared before the meeting.

____ 2. Participants have an opportunity to contribute to the agenda.

____ 3. The appropriate and necessary people attend each meeting.

____ 4. Those invited receive advance notice of the meeting time and place.

____ 5. Facilities are comfortable and adequate for the number of people attending.

____ 6. The meeting begins on time.

____ 7. The meeting has a scheduled ending time.

____ 8. The use of time is monitored throughout the meeting.

____ 9. Everyone has an opportunity to present his or her point of view.

____ 10. Participants listen attentively to each other.

____ 11. There are periodic summaries as the meeting progresses.

____ 12. The meeting is periodically evaluated by participants.

____ 13. No one tends to dominate the discussion.

____ 14. Everyone has a voice in decisions made at the meeting.

____ 15. The decision-making process used is appropriate for the size of the group.

CONTINUED

CONTINUED

____ 16. Audiovisual equipment is in good working condition.

____ 17. The meeting typically ends with a summary of accomplishments.

____ 18. People later carry out the actions agreed to during the meeting.

____ 19. Following the meeting, each participant receives minutes.

____ 20. The meeting leader follows up with participants.

Scoring

Number of Statements Checked _____ × 5 = _____ Meeting Score

High-quality meetings score 80 or above. A score below 60 suggests that the quality of the meetings you attend could be improved.

"Let's go around the room, and talk about the edgy, creative things we've done so far today."

Planning an Effective Meeting

As you can see from the previous pages, planning an effective meeting requires attention to detail. The following questions are a practical guide for your planning.

- Do you really need to meet?
- Will the meeting be an information meeting or a decision-making one?
- Do you need a face-to-face meeting, or will a virtual meeting work for you?
- What will be on the agenda?
- Who needs to attend?
- When and where will you meet?

To Meet or Not to Meet

Deciding on the type of meeting you need gives you a specific way to see what you want to accomplish. Before you go further in your planning, it is important to decide if you really need a meeting to accomplish your objectives. All too often, holding a meeting is a quick choice, when it should be a carefully considered decision.

What Are the Objectives?

The decision on whether to hold a meeting should start with a statement of objectives. What are the results you expect to achieve through a meeting? Is a meeting the best way to achieve those objectives?

Here are some examples of meeting objectives:

- To inform our department of changes in the holiday pay policy
- To sell management on our plans to attract a new type of customer
- To decide the best way to solve our organization's budget deficit
- To update all staff on the progress of a current project
- To determine realistic sales goals for each district based on the company's overall sales goals for next year
- To determine the critical skills required for successful performance as a first-level supervisor

With objectives clearly stated, you can then determine the best way to achieve them. It may turn out that a meeting is appropriate. Or it may turn out that an e-mail message, a memo, a bulletin board posting, or series of phone calls would be a better approach.

Types of Meetings

Meetings can be classified into two major types according to their purpose: information meetings and decision-making meetings. Each type has two subsets.

- ▶ Information meetings:
  - ▷ Advising and updating
  - ▷ Selling
- ▶ Decision-making meetings:
  - ▷ Goal and policy setting
  - ▷ Problem solving

These classifications are helpful because each type of meeting must be conducted differently.

Sometimes a meeting might combine both types. For example, if the meeting's purpose is to decide and create new policies, the first portion might be conducted as an information meeting, reviewing information the participants need for doing the work. The rest of the meeting would be conducted as a decision-making meeting.

THINK ABOUT IT

List three meetings you have attended or conducted recently. Were they information meetings, decision-making meetings, or both?

1. ______________________________
2. ______________________________
3. ______________________________

The chart on the next page lists more specific differences between the two meeting types. Use this chart to classify your meetings and then determine the proper way to plan for each type.

Which Type of Meeting Do You Need?

Elements	Information Meeting	Decision-Making Meeting
Number of attendees	Any number	Small size, preferably 12 or fewer people
Who should attend	Those who need to know	Those responsible and those who can contribute
Communication process	One way, from leader to participants, with opportunities for questions	Interactive discussion among all attending
Meeting room setup	Participants can face front of room, classroom style	Participants face each other, conference style
Most effective style of leadership	Authoritative	Participative
Emphasis should be	Content and answers to questions	Interaction and problem solving
Key to success	Planning and preparation of information to be presented	Meeting climate that supports open, free expression

Do You Really Need a Meeting?

For information meetings, use these criteria:

- ❑ Is time of the essence?
- ❑ Is the group geographically dispersed?
- ❑ Does the size of the group make a meeting feasible (10 to 100)?
- ❑ Is it imperative that everyone fully understand the information?
- ❑ Will the information presented be needed later as reference material?

For decision-making meetings, use these criteria:

- ❑ Is the knowledge required for problem solving dispersed among several people?
- ❑ Is the commitment of several people required for successful implementation of the results?
- ❑ Can the synergy of group interaction contribute to a good decision?
- ❑ Are there likely to be conflicting points of view that need to be reconciled?
- ❑ Are there questions of fairness that need to be resolved?

THINK ABOUT IT

List three meetings you have recently attended or conducted. Did you really need a meeting? Why or why not?

1. ______________________________
2. ______________________________
3. ______________________________

Face-to-Face or Virtual?

Telephones, video, and computers all provide options for the "virtual meeting," allowing people to meet and share information without being together in the same place. Virtual meetings can save time and money. They can provide a cost-effective way for people to share information, ideas, discussions, and planning.

There are three types of virtual meetings, based on the technology used. Here is an overview.

Teleconferences

Teleconferencing, the oldest of the virtual meeting formats, has been around since the days of the party telephone line. When three or more neighbors were visiting on the party line, they were participating in some of the first conference calls.

Today's teleconferencing has come a long way from the old party line. The technology works well for simple information sharing and straightforward decision-making meetings that require no visual presentation. It is not a suitable venue for discussing more complicated matters. Also, teleconferencing is not a desirable way either to begin or to further important relationships. However, given its limitations, it can still accomplish a lot.

Computer Conferences

The Internet makes it possible for people to communicate inexpensively, in real time. Depending on the software application used, a computer conference can provide video, text, and voice communication. Geographically dispersed people can then share information, collaborate, and solve problems.

Another feature of the Internet that supports and facilitates meetings is the ability to create an *extranet*. This is a private Web site that allows people who have access to share files and use message boards. While these features cannot take the place of a meeting, they can be used quite effectively to share information in advance of either a traditional or virtual meeting. And through ongoing communication and document sharing, they may actually reduce the need for some meetings.

Will a Virtual Meeting Work for You?

Before setting up a virtual meeting, decide if that is the best way to accomplish what you need to do. Virtual meetings are not for everyone. They work best when you have a group of people who already know each other. It is also useful to get together for some face-to-face time every now and then because face-to-face meetings provide a different type of interaction. Following are some of the advantages and disadvantages of virtual meetings.

Advantages

The advantages of virtual meetings can include:

- **Cost savings** — The cost of travel has increased substantially. With the savings from travel offset against equipment costs, virtual meetings can easily be the less costly way to get together.
- **Time savings** — Virtual meetings are usually shorter meetings. There is less social interaction, and meetings tend to be more structured and focused.
- **Setup speed** — When the need to arrange travel is removed, the lead time required to convene a meeting is reduced dramatically.
- **Broad reach** — Virtual meetings can pass information on to a very large number of people at the same time. Videoconferencing and some forms of computer conferencing are particularly well suited to this type of communication.

Disadvantages

The disadvantages of virtual meetings can include:

- **Less group cohesiveness** — Virtual meetings do not facilitate group development. People can't share anxieties, concerns, plans, and problems in the same way they do in face-to-face gatherings. The process of going to a meeting and mingling with others can confirm organizational culture and team spirit in a way that virtual meetings cannot.
- **Reduced impact** — A new product or service can be introduced by way of a virtual meeting. But the excitement and feedback opportunities available when everyone is in the same place at the same time will be missing.
- **Elimination of informal exchange** — The informal exchange that takes place at face-to-face meetings is often as useful as the official agenda. People who may hardly ever see each other can talk over organizational problems and potentials. For most virtual meetings, this component is not available.
- **Dilution of message** — Virtual meetings depend on a variety of technologies and limit the way in which you can present and exchange information. In addition, some people might become so absorbed in the technology that they miss the message being presented. Some people believe that these limitations alter the impact and the value of the information.

THINK ABOUT IT

If you have attended a virtual meeting, do you think it worked well? Why or why not?

Can you think of a meeting topic in your organization that would be well suited for a virtual meeting?

Why do you think it would work?

Developing an Agenda

When you have decided to have a meeting and decided what type of meeting to have, your next step is to develop an agenda. Every meeting should have an agenda, and participants should get it in advance, if possible. In most cases, participants should have an opportunity to contribute to the agenda before the meeting. A combination of e-mail and phone calls is usually effective for developing an agenda with input from at least some of the participants. An agenda need not be an elaborate document, but it should be specific and should be documented in some visible form—as a handout, on a slide, on a board, or on a flip chart.

The needs of the participants are an important guide when you prepare a published agenda. What do they need to know to effectively participate in the meeting? The following elements should be included:

- Date and time of meeting
- Objectives
- Items to be discussed (listed in proper sequence)
- Adjournment time
- Time of scheduled breaks, if any

Example of a Meeting Agenda

- Opening statement: reason for attendance, objective, time commitment
- Problems to be discussed (list, if more than one)
- Generate solutions
- Decide among alternatives
- Develop plan to solve problem(s)
- Assign tasks to carry out plan
- Establish follow-up procedures
- Summarize and adjourn

Other Agenda Considerations

When you are planning or leading a meeting, there are other agenda-related details you'll need to consider. Paying attention to these will help ensure that your agenda is an effective tool.

The Leader's Agenda

As leader, you need more detail than the participants. For example, you should have an approximate time allocation for each item to properly gauge the progress of the meeting. Also, you may need notes on techniques to use, points to clarify, and equipment that may be required.

Sending the Agenda

When sending an agenda before a meeting, think about who should receive a copy. Determine who should receive a copy strictly for information and who you expect to attend and participate in the meeting. Address your transmittal to those you expect to attend. Show the information-only recipients as cc's. This will clear up any uncertainty about who is expected to attend.

Sending the agenda ahead of time allows participants to think and prepare for the meeting. You can get your agenda out by e-mail, by posting it in a visible place, or by written memo. It usually works best if each person has a copy. Be sure to have extra copies at the meeting for people who forget to bring theirs.

For Regular Meetings

Regularly scheduled staff or committee meetings seem to be the most common violators of the agenda requirement. One way to overcome this problem is to take five minutes at the beginning of the meeting to develop and post an agenda. If there are several items on the agenda, prioritize them so you can deal with the most important ones in the time available. If new items come up during the meeting, add them to the agenda in proper priority order.

THINK ABOUT IT

What does an agenda contribute to the effectiveness of a meeting?

____

____

Selecting Participants

When you're selecting meeting participants, the best guideline is to have the smallest number of appropriate people. This is not always easy. There often will be people who think they should come, but they are unable to contribute and will not gain from attendance. Also, there may be people you think you should invite because of their position in the organization, but they, too, may have nothing to contribute.

The only feasible method for selecting participants is to consider the type of meeting you are planning.

- For an information meeting, you want attendees who need to know the information being presented or who will contribute to presenting the information.
- For a problem-solving meeting, you need participants who have knowledge to contribute, authority over the area affected by the decision, and/or the commitment to carry out the decision.

Before the meeting, give some thought to those who might wish to attend but are not on your participant list. To maintain good relationships, it may be wise to explain the objective of your meeting to them and state why you think they do not need to attend. They will probably react in one of the following ways:

- Agreeing with you and thanking you for your thoughtfulness
- Disagreeing with you and presenting reasons that might cause you to change your mind
- Disagreeing with you but requiring you to stand firm on their exclusion

Criteria for Information Meeting Attendees

For deciding who should attend an information meeting, use these criteria:

- **Need to know the information** — Attendees should be people who will need to use the information or who will be affected by it.
- **Need to receive the information at the same time** — Some people might not need the information immediately, and can get it later in some other reliable way. If so, these people do not need to attend the meeting.
- **Ability to ask important, useful questions** — The question-and-answer session has a lot to do with the success of an information meeting. People who can contribute to it effectively will help achieve the goal of the meeting.
- **Ability to support the implementation of the information** — If there are people who will be key in implementing the information, you might want them to attend the meeting.

Criteria for Problem-Solving Meeting Attendees

For deciding who should attend a problem-solving meeting, use these criteria:

- **Knowledge of the subject area** — You need people who represent the various aspects of the expertise required to develop a valid solution to the problem.
- **Commitment to solving the problem** — Group members should have a vested interest in solving the problem.
- **Time to participate** — Each person must have time to participate in problem-solving activities.
- **Diversity of viewpoints** — The group must be able to look at a problem in different ways to avoid patterned thinking.
- **Expressiveness** — Group members must feel free to express facts, opinions, and feelings.
- **Open-mindedness** — When members are willing to listen to each other, and to change their minds when they are convinced by compelling arguments, they can reach the best solution.

THINK ABOUT IT

Have you attended meetings where authority to make a decision was missing? What was the impact on the meeting?

Have you attended meetings where more people were present than were needed? What was the impact on the meeting?

Have you attended meetings where important knowledge was missing? What was the impact on the meeting?

Notifying Participants

When you invite people to a meeting, you need to send them the information they will need to be able to attend, take part, and deal with their need for food and other accommodations if necessary. The following checklist summarizes things most participants need to know in order to attend and participate in a meeting. Use it as a model for your meetings.

For all participants:

- ❑ Meeting date and time
- ❑ Location
- ❑ Directions
- ❑ Agenda
- ❑ Any advance work they need to do
- ❑ Any material they need to bring
- ❑ Proper attire
- ❑ Parking arrangements if necessary
- ❑ Meal arrangements if necessary
- ❑ Whom to contact to request accommodations for disabilities

Additional items for out-of-town participants:

- ❑ Travel arrangements
- ❑ Accommodation arrangements
- ❑ Billing instructions for items such as:
    - ❑ Travel
    - ❑ Hotel
    - ❑ Meals
    - ❑ Parking

Choosing a Meeting Time

Certain days of the week and selected times of the day are better than others for holding meetings. Give careful thought to your meeting time so that participants can be present, on time, and ready to engage in the business of the meeting.

When choosing a meeting time, consider the following:

- **Preparation time** — How much time will it take you and the participants to do the necessary preparation work?
- **Your availability** — If you are leading the meeting, or need to be a participant, what time will work for you?
- **Facilities** — When will an appropriate and comfortable meeting space, with the facilities and equipment you need, be available?
- **Participant availability** — What options for meeting times do your participants have? Current office software suites often include message programs that make this step much easier.

When choosing a time to meet, avoid late afternoons before a holiday or weekend, and avoid early mornings following a day off. Be willing to be creative. For example, consider meeting during the noon hour with a brown-bag lunch, or before the start of the official workday with a continental breakfast.

Meetings of groups such as civic associations or professional societies must meet outside of normal work hours. They face more of a challenge finding an acceptable meeting time. These sessions will typically fall in the evening during the week. If you are part of a small group, explore the possibility of meeting at other times acceptable to all involved, such as various weekend or meal times. Remember, if facilities are available and everyone is willing to meet, any time is acceptable.

Think About It

What are some examples of meetings you attended that met at unconventional times? Did the meeting time have any bearing on the meeting's effectiveness?

____

____

Dealing with Common Meeting Problems

This list is an overview of specific steps you can take toward holding more effective meetings. Check (√) those you most want to implement or improve.

- ☐ **State your objective.**

  Every meeting needs objectives. They should be clearly presented in the leader's opening statement. This simple procedure establishes the reason for the meeting. With an objective in mind, participants can direct their discussion and energy to that goal.

- ☐ **Prepare an agenda.**

  An agenda is essential. You should prepare one and give it to participants in advance. It will serve as a road map to keep discussion on the topic. When distributed before a meeting, an agenda encourages advance preparation.

- ☐ **Manage the meeting time.**

  Strike a balance between wasting time and railroading the group. Allow sufficient time for participants to become involved and feel satisfied with the outcome. Start on time and keep things moving toward an announced ending time.

- ☐ **Take charge.**

  Effective control and guidance are required for effective meetings. Use the agenda to keep the discussion on topic. Encourage less active participants to contribute. Control those who attempt to dominate. Determine ahead of time the best procedures for achieving the meeting's objective, and use them at appropriate times.

- ☐ **Close with a summary.**

  Every meeting should close with a restatement of the meeting's objective, a summary of what was accomplished toward the objective, and a review of any agreed-upon action that needs to be taken.

Part Summary

In this part, you learned how to define and plan an effective meeting. You learned about the types of meetings, and learned that they can be conducted face-to-face or in a virtual format. You learned how to develop an agenda. Then, you learned how to select and notify participants, and how best to choose a meeting time. Finally, you learned how to address some common meeting problems.

P A R T 2

Facilities and Equipment

"*Effective meetings don't happen by accident, they happen by design.*"

–Anonymous

In this part:

- Facility and Equipment Guidelines
- Meeting Room Checklist
- Guidelines for Visual Aids
- Projection Methods
- Arranging Virtual Meetings
- Conference Calls
- Online Conferencing

Facility and Equipment Guidelines

The meeting room, furnishings, and equipment will contribute significantly to an effective meeting. When facilities are effective, they go unnoticed. When they are inadequate or too elaborate, they can detract from the meeting.

Choosing On-Site or Off-Site

On-site meeting rooms are usually convenient and low cost. This makes them attractive considerations. However, being convenient for participants also makes them convenient for interruptions. Occasionally, an on-site room will not be the right size for a particular meeting. Be willing to look elsewhere for a proper meeting place.

Planning for Physical Comfort and Special Needs

Pay attention to participants' physical comfort. Chairs should be comfortable, especially if the meeting will last over an hour. Heating and cooling, lighting, and ventilation should be adequate for the size of the group and the activities planned. You may also need to consider adaptations and space if any people attending have disabilities.

Providing Tables

A table is required only when it has a use (for example, to write on or to spread out maps, charts, and computer printouts). While tables are standard in most meeting rooms, consider your need. Perhaps a better room arrangement would be available without a table. However, if you want participants to take notes, or if you know some will be bringing laptops, provide tables for comfortable writing.

Setting Up the Room

When setting up the room, consider the communication needs for the type of meeting you plan to hold. Usually, you want people talking with each other to maintain eye contact. Therefore, information meetings should have participants facing the front of the room, if that will be the best way for them to see the speaker. For a smaller group, you can use a U-shape. Decision-making meetings should have participants facing each other. Examples of different room arrangements are shown on the following pages.

Sample Room Arrangement 1 for Information Meeting

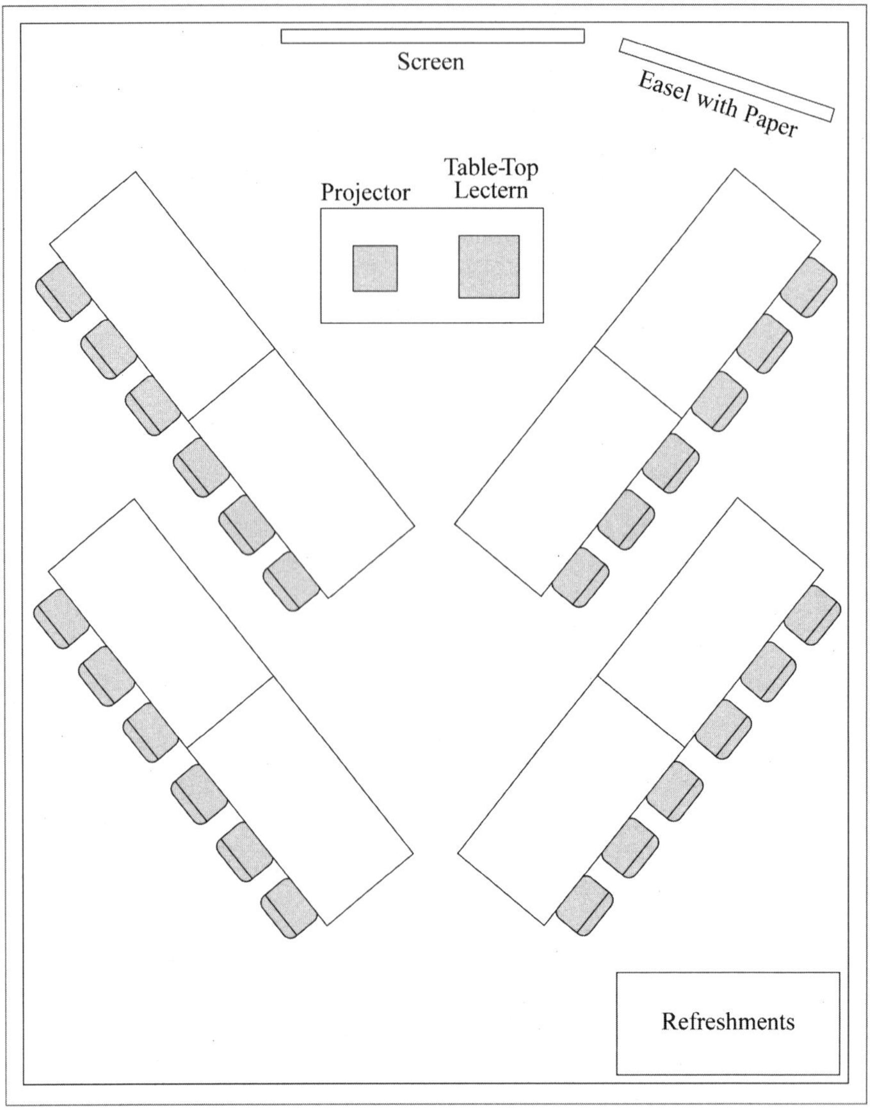

Sample Room Arrangement 2 for Information Meeting

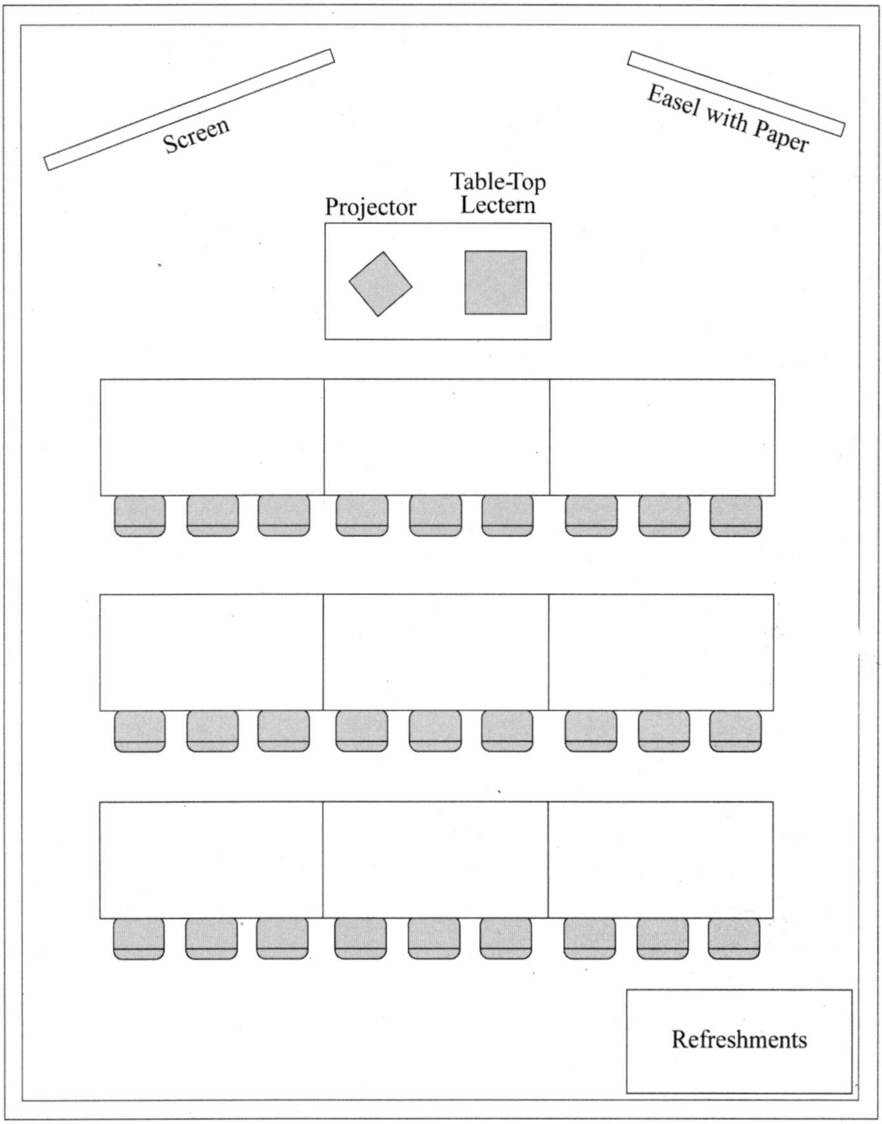

Sample Room Arrangement for Either Type of Meeting

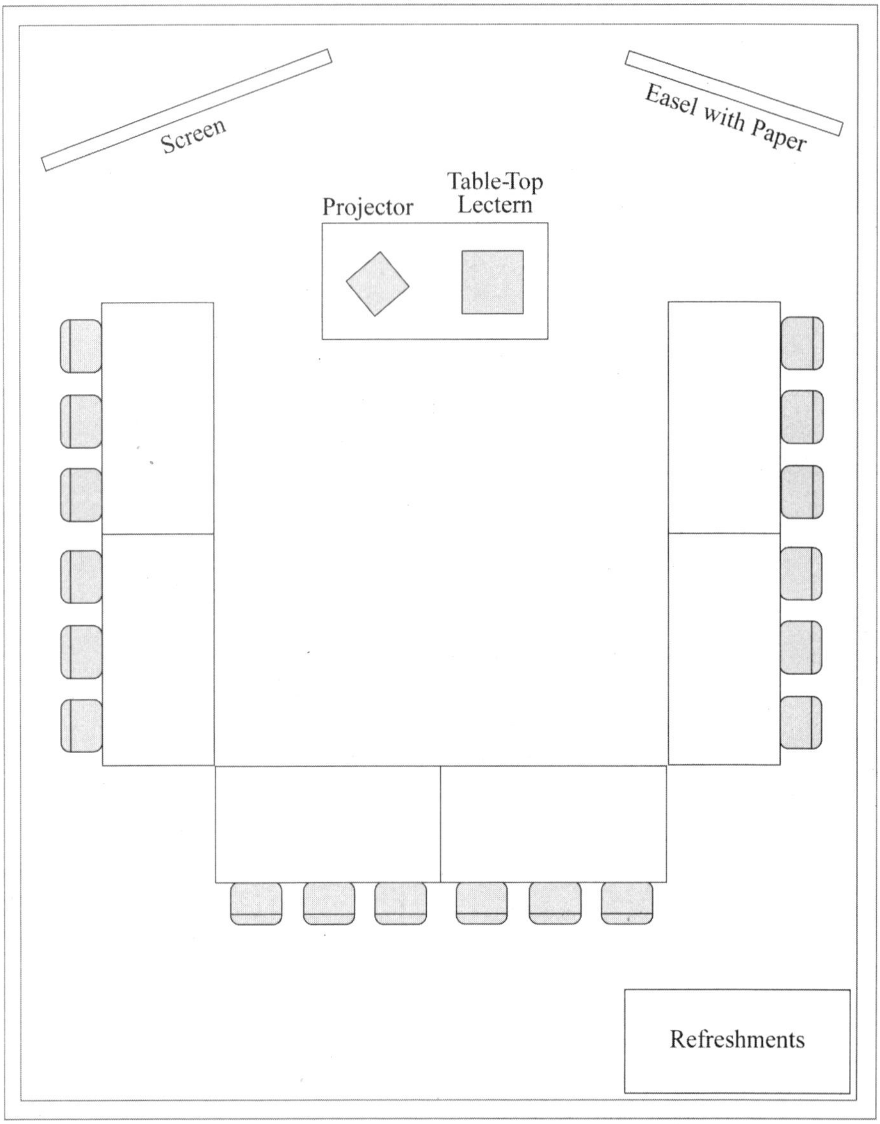

Sample Room Arrangement 1 for Decision-Making Meeting

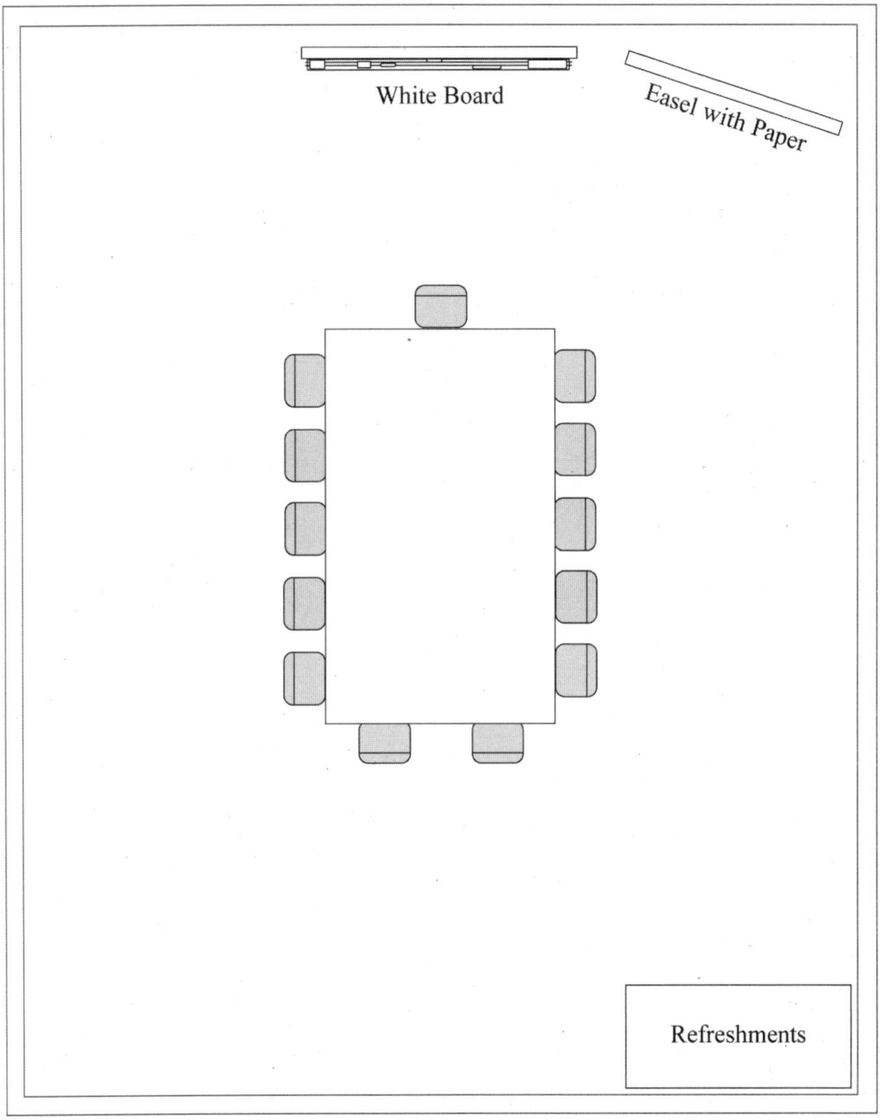

Sample Room Arrangement 2 for Decision-Making Meeting

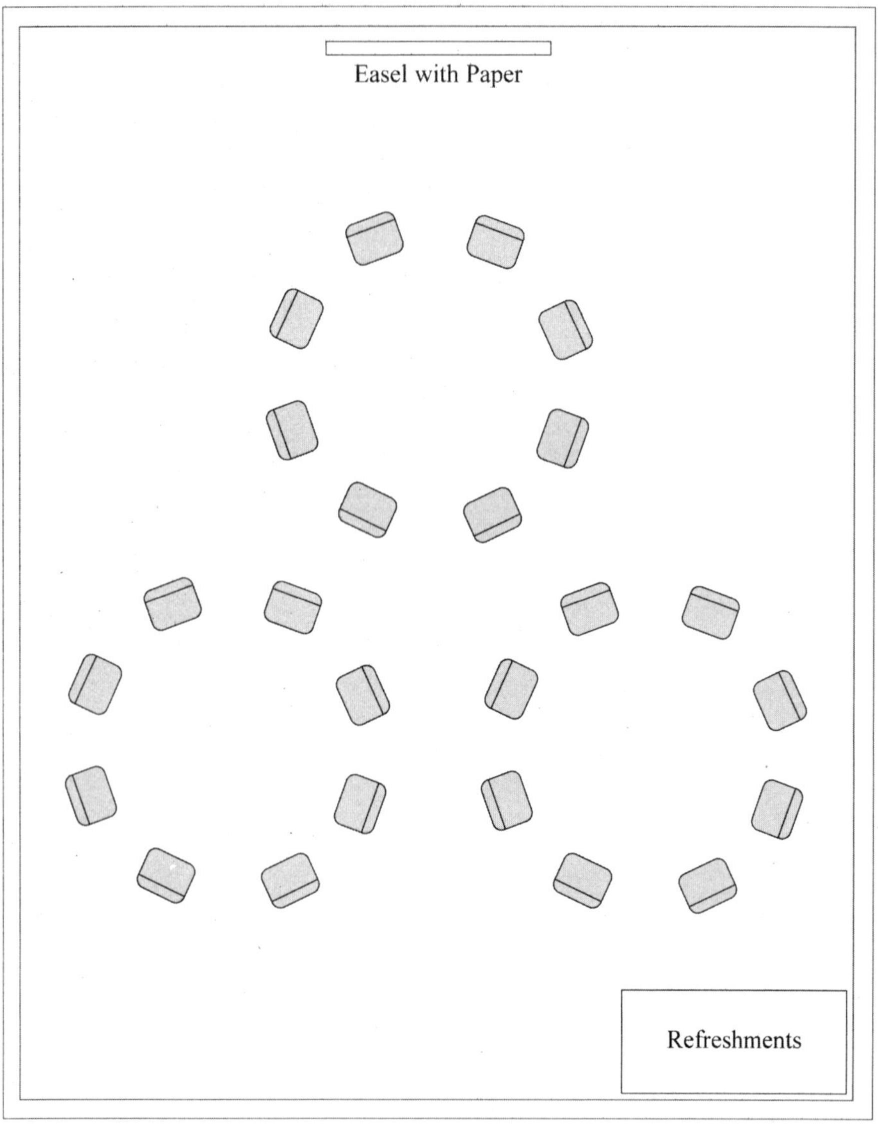

Meeting Room Checklist

The following checklist summarizes the key requirements for an acceptable meeting room. Use it to see if a potential meeting room will meet your needs.

- ❑ Is the room large enough to comfortably accommodate the participants and any audiovisual aids or equipment?
- ❑ Is there adequate lighting and ventilation? Can they be controlled from within the room?
- ❑ Is the room free from distractions and interruptions, such as telephones, loud noises, or other activities?
- ❑ Is the room appropriately furnished? Are the chairs comfortable enough for the length of the meeting?
- ❑ Will the room accommodate participants with disabilities?
- ❑ Is the room conveniently located for participants?
- ❑ Is the cost of the room within budget?
- ❑ Is the room available at the time you need it?

THINK ABOUT IT

Think of a meeting you attended recently. Did the facilities work well? If so, in what way? If not, what could have been done to make them more effective?

Think of a meeting room or conference room that gets a lot of use in your office or organization. What things could you change that would improve the space for any future meetings in that room?

Guidelines for Visual Aids

Well-designed visual aids are helpful in both information and decision-making meetings. Today, the most common type of visual aid is a computerized slide presentation, such as Microsoft PowerPoint, although flip charts or overhead transparencies are still viable options. Visual aids should help guide the meeting—*not* become the entire focus of the meeting. Use visual aids to:

- Stay focused on key points
- Simplify complex content
- Focus attention on discussion points
- Display graphs, data, pictures, drawings, or illustrations

Designing Visual Aids

When creating visual aids:

- Use a white, soft blue, or light gray background.
- Use large letters, and avoid using all caps (which is too difficult to read).
- Use a simple type style, and only one or two fonts.
- Use no more than two colors that contrast with the background.
- Use no more than six lines per visual.
- Use no more than four to six words per line.

Tip: Slides should support your presentation in outline form and should not include every detail. To provide your audience with in-depth information, distribute handouts, but not until *after* the presentation.

THINK ABOUT IT

Think about meetings you have attended recently. Did you see visuals that were well presented and that made their point clearly? What made them work well?

Think of a topic you might present at a meeting. What points would be good to put into visuals? Draft some ideas in the boxes below.

Projection Methods

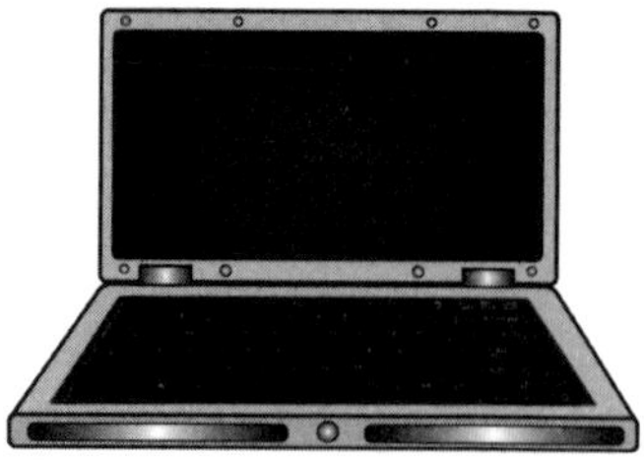

At many business meetings, a presenter uses a laptop computer connected to an LCD projector to display presentation software to the attendees. Presentation software displays slides or other images that can include text, graphics, and animation.

Ensuring a Stress-free Laptop Presentation

Before a meeting, do the following:

- **Check the computer** — Whether using your own computer or one provided at the meeting site, run through your presentation on it before the meeting.
- **Get a remote mouse** — Using a remote mouse will free you to stand away from your computer and move about the meeting room.
- **Turn off the screen saver** — It is very distracting if it comes on during your presentation.
- **Back up your material** — Put another copy of the presentation in a different folder on your hard drive. Then put yet another copy on a CD, DVD, or flash drive.
- **Back up your presentation** — Have another laptop available in the room in case yours fails. You can also use transparencies with an overhead projector as a backup if a second laptop is not available.

Other Projection Methods

If an LCD projector is not available, see if an overhead projector or even a 35mm slide projector is available. A business services provider can transfer your presentation slides or document file to transparencies or slides. This method can be costly and time-consuming, however.

When you display information, participants may focus on the visual rather than on the speaker. If the visuals become too distracting, you may want to turn off the projector after a slide has been presented so people can focus on the discussion. If you have a small meeting, and simple information to convey with visuals (no illustrations or complex graphs), you might consider simply using a prepared flip chart.

Whatever projection method you decide to use, be sure to practice using it ahead of time to avoid glitches during the meeting.

Guidelines for Projector Screens

There are a few simple guidelines for the proper placement of screens and projectors, room orientation, and screen size that contribute to an effective meeting.

- Everyone in the room must have a clear view of the screen. The speaker and projector must not obstruct the view of the screen.
- Place the screen to the speaker's right (if right-handed) to allow easy access for pointing or writing.
- Matte-finish screens provide a clear image when viewed at angles down to 25 degrees. Beaded and lenticular screens do not perform well at this sharp of an angle.
- The speaker should be located at one end of a room's narrow dimension.
- Focus the LCD projector. Adjust the projector or the laptop to compensate for a type of image distortion known as keystoning, so that the screen displays a square image. If these methods don't work, try tilting the screen slightly backward or forward.
- The proper size of a screen is determined by the distance to the person seated furthest from it. See the table below.

Distance to screen (feet)	**20**	**25**	**30**	**35**	**40**
Screen size (inches)	50 × 50	60 × 60	70 × 70	84 × 84	96 × 96

Equipment Checklist

Whatever type of visuals you use, be sure to have the proper equipment and to check it all carefully before you start. Here is a suggested checklist you can use.

- ❑ Screen placed so that all participants can see it easily and clearly
- ❑ Screen placed to the speaker's right or left, depending on the speaker's preference, to allow easy access for changing visuals or writing
- ❑ Projector focused and adjusted to eliminate image distortion as much as possible
- ❑ Screen size that works well for the size of the room
- ❑ Projection equipment conveniently placed for speaker
- ❑ Extra bulbs for slide or overhead projector
- ❑ Extension cords and power strips as needed
- ❑ Tape for taping down cords
- ❑ Laser pointer if needed by speaker
- ❑ Remote mouse
- ❑ Backup CD, DVD, or flash drive

"I like to have meetings where we can all talk freely without fear of being spied upon."

Arranging Virtual Meetings

When arranging a virtual meeting, you need to pay even more attention to facilities and, especially, to the equipment. You have a tightly specified time for your meeting, you are connected to people in other locations and probably other time zones, and any equipment problem will result in lost time, frustration, and perhaps the need to reschedule. Consider the following guidelines:

- Select a room away from noise and distractions. When you are listening on the phone or via computer or video broadcast, noise from outside makes it harder to hear participants. The noise might also be carried to the other meeting locations over the equipment.
- If several people are participating from a shared location, have ample space for participants to sit comfortably, where they can hear and see well, take notes, and share equipment as needed.
- Get information, documents, and any other needed material to participants well ahead of time, so you do not use valuable meeting time distributing these things.
- Check all equipment ahead of time. If you set it up a day or more ahead, check it again just before the meeting starts.
- Because some of the participants will be present only by phone, video, or computer, be sure to set up a meeting protocol in advance to ensure that all participants can have their say.

Conference Calls

Perhaps the easiest form of virtual meeting is the telephone conference call. You may already have taken part in this kind of meeting. In many larger organizations, conference call capability is already part of the telephone system, at least in some conference rooms and/or work areas. Many basic phone packages come with the option to bring at least a third person into a conversation. Most telephone companies offer teleconference services and can help you choose and install equipment if it is not available already.

Basic Formats for Conference Calls

There are three basic formats: distributed group, one-to-group, and group-to-group.

Distributed Group

This type of meeting works well when the people who need to communicate are located in a variety of locations. Many office telephone systems already provide this feature. If yours does not, your telephone company may provide this service. Finally, a quick Web search will return dozens of companies that offer this service, sometimes free of charge. At the time scheduled for the call, participants call the number you provide, enter a participant code, and are connected to the conference.

One-to-Group

Another format used for conference calls is to convene a face-to-face meeting in a room that has a speaker phone. Then, one or two people call in from another location. This format is effective when the input of one person is essential to a group's problem solving or decision making. It facilitates two-way communication so that everyone in the meeting can fully understand the input of the remotely located person. This format is also effective for information meetings, such as briefing sessions.

Group-to-Group

The third format ties two face-to-face meetings together. Each meeting room has teleconferencing equipment, including adequate speakers and microphones. Everyone taking part can hear all that is said in both locations and can speak to both locations. This type of virtual meeting can be effective for sharing ideas between two groups. It can also be used for simple problem solving and decision making with groups that already know each other.

Dealing with Common Conference Call Problems

To prevent problems during conference calls, consider the following:

- **Noise** — Choose a meeting space that cuts out as much outside noise as possible. The acoustics of the meeting environment can be a major problem for conference calls. Background noise will be picked up on microphones and interfere with sound quality. Also, room design can contribute to echoing that produces further interference.
- **Leadership** — A conference call, like any other meeting, requires leadership to be effective. The leader should ensure that everyone has an opportunity to participate. You might want to set up the speaking order ahead of time or rotate through participants in a specific pattern. Be sure to call on each person at least once during the meeting. At the end, be sure that everyone has a chance to add further comments if needed.
- **Speaking order** — In face-to-face meetings, people can use visual signals to determine who will speak next. There are no such signals in a phone call. This can be handled in several ways. In the group session of a one-to-group call, and in both sessions of a group-to-group call, a moderator can direct the order of speaking. Conference calls usually have few enough participants that this is not a problem. In addition, it may be helpful if participants who don't know one another identify themselves when they speak.
- **Printed materials** — Remember to send out printed materials in advance. You can use e-mail, faxes, postal mail, or shipping.

THINK ABOUT IT

Have you ever taken part in a conference call? Did it work well for you? For the other participants?

____

____

Could anything have been done to improve the meeting? If so, what?

____

____

Online Conferencing

Internet access provides a number of ways to share information, ideas, documents, and conversation. Internet providers, as well as companies that specialize in Web conferencing or interactive online meeting services, provide a variety of services related to computer conferencing. Intranets and extranets also facilitate this kind of computer conferencing. Computer conferencing offers a great deal of flexibility. It can be used for instant text messaging (also called chatting), audio, video, file sharing, file editing, and screen sharing.

Basic Formats for Computer Conferencing

There are several basic formats: point-to-point, multicast, multipoint, and Web conferencing.

Point-to-Point

A point-to-point conference involves two locations. Participants at each location are equipped for both speaking and sharing information visually. Video cameras can be set up so that participants can see each other as well as the information they are sharing. This format is effective for collaboration and information sharing between people in two locations. The simplest form of computer conferencing uses the built-in microphone and camera in many of today's computers.

Multicast

A multicast originates with one person and is received by other people at various locations. Communication flows back and forth between the originator and the recipients, but not between recipients. Using a desktop computer, these conferences can be audio only or audio and video. The audio stream can be augmented by visuals on the computer monitor. This format works well for disseminating information and can be used effectively in educational settings.

Multipoint

Multipoint conferences work the same way as point-to-point conferences, but several locations are involved. This format can be used effectively for sharing information, problem solving, and elementary decision making.

Web Conferencing

Web conferencing services, such as WebEx.com or GoToMeeting.com, provide the easiest and most cost-effective way to organize and attend online meetings. The technology these services provide allows participants to view any application running on your computer in real time, and it combines real-time desktop sharing with phone conferencing so everyone sees the same thing as you talk.

Dealing with Common Conference Problems

Video quality: The quality of visual information shared over the Web depends largely on the quality of the Internet connections and the quality of the participants' monitors. If participants are using cameras, the video quality of those images also depends largely on the equipment.

Audio quality: If participants are using phones for speaking with each other, the audio quality is usually reasonably good. Audio sent via computer speakers is usually quite good, although it can fall short of normal telephone standards. Remember that with long-distance transmission, brief time delays might occur. Quality is often better when a conference call provides the audio.

Cost: Internet and intranet connections are now common in most organizations. The software needed for information exchanges via the Web often comes with office suite software. If the participants use telephones for discussion, the cost for that is the same as for any telephone conference. There are additional costs for cameras and high-quality speakers.

Firewall: Some firewalls might create computer-conferencing problems. If you run into a problem, or think it might be a problem before you start, consult your organization's IT group or contact technical support for your firewall software.

Bandwidth: Bandwidth can be an issue. Video can be a resource hog, and this creates problems for both Internet links and intranets. Some organizations, particularly smaller ones, are finding that when everyone starts using computer conferencing, their present capacity is not sufficient. Telephone and Internet service companies can usually help with this problem.

Confidentiality: Today's office environment poses potential risks to keeping certain information confidential. As with all computer use, virtual meetings can create confidentiality problems. The solutions are the same as for any computer security: care in who sees, sends, and receives material; care in who might overhear discussions; and care in the use of passwords.

THINK ABOUT IT

Have you ever taken part in a computer conference? Did it work well for you? For the other participants?

____

____

Could anything have been done to improve the meeting? If so, what?

____

____

Checklist for Virtual Meetings

When you set up a virtual meeting, pay attention to the same considerations you think of when setting up any kind of meeting, plus a few more, as indicated on this checklist.

- ❑ All equipment arranged, several days ahead of time
- ❑ All equipment in place and checked before the meeting
- ❑ For a conference call, all arrangements made for participants to call in as scheduled
- ❑ All needed material and instructions sent to participants ahead of time
- ❑ If participants will meet in a specific room: room comfortably set up with ample space for the equipment needed
- ❑ Meeting room away from noise and other distractions
- ❑ If participants will be using computers: computers and software checked ahead of time for compatibility
- ❑ Extra equipment available in case any equipment fails
- ❑ Technical support available in case problems arise during meeting

Part Summary

In this part, you learned how to set up for a meeting. You learned about facility and equipment guidelines, and you learned how best to use LCD projectors and other visual aids. You learned how to set up virtual meetings, including conference calls and online conferencing, and how to address common problems with each format.

P A R T 3

Conducting Meetings

"Meetings without an agenda are like a restaurant without a menu."

–Susan B. Wilson

In this part:

- The Meeting Leader's Role
- Major Components of a Meeting
- Structuring Information Meetings
- Structuring Decision-Making Meetings
- Criteria-Based Rating
- Criteria-Based Ranking

The Meeting Leader's Role

As leader, you must focus the energy and attention of participants and keep them moving toward the meeting's objectives. This can be a complex task.

To be effective, you must be able to:

- Stay focused and keep the group focused.
- Analyze each situation.
- Determine what is needed to move forward.
- Take the necessary action to achieve the objectives.

Setting Meeting Ground Rules

One of the first things you can do to help ensure meeting effectiveness is to establish ground rules specifying how participants are to behave. Behavior in meetings is based on experience. From their experiences, people make assumptions about what is proper. The way to deal with these assumptions is to set ground rules.

As meeting leader, you may set these rules yourself, or you may set them through discussion and agreement with participants. If the meeting is a one-time event, the first approach is suggested. If the same participants meet regularly, a participative approach might be better.

With a group that has met for several sessions, ask the question: "What do we typically do in our meetings?" Then classify what is identified as either detracting from or contributing to the group's effectiveness. (Some things can be dropped as inconsequential.) Finally, develop ground rules to overcome detracting behavior and reinforce contributing behavior. Ground rules can be set in the areas of content, interaction, and/or structure.

Examples of meeting ground rules:

- The meeting will begin on time.
- Group members will help set the meeting agenda.
- Participants will raise their hands rather than jumping in or interrupting someone.
- Decisions will be made by consensus.
- Conflict is okay.
- Expression of feelings and opinions is encouraged.

Practice Setting Meeting Ground Rules

Consider a group you meet with regularly. Think of things that typically happen and classify them as either detracting from or contributing to group effectiveness. Then draw up some tentative ground rules around these behaviors.

Detracting Behavior	Contributing Behavior

Ground rules to overcome detracting behavior and reinforce contributing behavior:

1. ______________________________
2. ______________________________
3. ______________________________
4. ______________________________
5. ______________________________
6. ______________________________
7. ______________________________

Major Components of a Meeting

As a meeting leader, you can understand your multifaceted role better if you understand the three major components of a meeting:

- **Content** — The information, knowledge, experience, opinions, ideas, myths, attitudes, and expectations that participants bring to the meeting.
- **Interaction** — The way participants work together while processing the meeting's content. Interaction includes feelings, attitudes, and expectations that bear on cooperation, listening, participation, trust, and openness.
- **Structure** — The way in which both information and participants are organized to achieve the meeting's purpose.

An effective leader is attentive to each of these components. The meeting leader's role is to monitor progress and provide necessary direction. In some meetings, participants help provide direction, making the leader's job easier. In other meetings, the leader is required to provide most of the direction.

The chart following the "Think About It" exercise outlines activities that might be appropriate for each component of a meeting.

THINK ABOUT IT

How will knowing about the three components of a meeting help you as a meeting leader?

Activities Involved in Conducting a Meeting

The leader's role is to monitor the activity in each key component area and provide the missing elements required to move the group toward the meeting's objectives.

Content	Interaction	Structure
Initiate action Keep on topic Elicit information Compare viewpoints Summarize Test for decision Develop action plans	Monitor participation Encourage participation Model supportive behavior Encourage building and supporting Encourage differing and confronting Facilitate conflict resolution Explore reactions and feelings Facilitate feedback	Develop agenda State objectives Manage time Record and display data Analyze data Generate alternatives Assign roles Develop ground rules

"I thought we'd start with the basics."

Structuring Information Meetings

Information meetings need structure to ensure that participants receive the information accurately and completely and that they get their questions answered. An information meeting works well when it has a structure similar to this:

1. Introduction of the leader or leaders, and their positions relevant to the meeting's purpose
2. An overview of the meeting's purpose
3. A well-structured presentation of the information
4. An orderly and informative question-and-answer session
5. Information for participants on what will happen next
6. Information for participants on how to get answers to further questions

Questions to Ask in Preparing for an Information Meeting

To prepare for an information meeting, consider the following:

- What information do participants need about the meeting topic?
- How much information do they need to have?
- Why do participants need the information—what will they do with it?
- Would it be better to have one meeting for the entire group, or several smaller meetings?
- Would it be useful to send out some of the information ahead of time? If so, how and when will participants receive the advance information?
- Who can best present this information?
- Who will conduct the question-and-answer session?
- What types of questions do you anticipate?
- What will participants do with the information after they leave the meeting?
- Will further meetings be needed?

Presenting Information Effectively

Because the primary purpose of an information meeting is to present information, it is critical that you present that information effectively. You want the participants to understand the information, to see how it applies to them and how it affects them, and to leave the meeting feeling that they know what is happening in relation to your topic.

Here is a suggested outline for presenting information effectively:

1. Opening remarks

   The opening remarks should state clearly the topic of the meeting, why this topic is important for those attending, and what the participants can expect from the meeting.

2. Overview

   After the opening, present an overview or outline of the material, showing the key points that will be covered during the meeting.

3. Organization of the information

   Organize your information in some logical sequence. Consider using a timeline or a list of priorities, or starting with the information that will have the most impact. Refer frequently to the outline so participants can see where you are going and what has already been covered.

4. Relation of the information to the participants

   As you go through the presentation, explain clearly what this information means to participants: how it will affect them and what they will be doing or not doing with the information.

5. Summary of main points

   As you come to the end of your presentation, review what you have covered in the main points.

6. Information on follow-up

   Explain to the participants what will happen next, what they can expect, and what is expected of them.

Question-and-Answer Sessions

The question-and-answer session is an important part of the information meeting. People might want to get more details, learn more about how the information will affect them, or get clarification on certain points.

It is important to build structure and order into these sessions. Otherwise, they can become too long, too short, or chaotic. People can get frustrated about not getting their individual questions answered, or the behavior of some of the participants may be annoying or even disruptive.

Conduct a Question-and-Answer Session That Works

Here are some things you can do to ensure productive Q&A sessions:

1. Anticipate questions. Think ahead about what participants might ask, so you can be prepared to answer. Perhaps building some of the answers into the presentation itself would be effective.
2. Introduce the person who will answer questions, if different from the presenter, and explain that person's relevance.
3. Announce the time allotted for the session. Tell participants how much time will be devoted to questions and answers. In addition, explain what participants can do to get answers if there is no time for their individual questions.
4. Lay ground rules. Explain how you will take questions. Ask participants to raise their hands, and tell them if they need to stand or use a microphone when asking their questions.
5. Repeat the question before answering it. Often, for a variety of reasons, some participants will not hear the question. Repeating the questions also gives the participant a chance to clarify a question if needed.
6. At the end of the allotted time, thank participants for taking part. Explain again how they can get answers for questions not answered or for questions they think of later.

Structuring Decision-Making Meetings

Decision-making meetings need structure in order to keep attention focused on the problem. Structure will help maintain the discipline of problem solving. For example, some participants may come to the meeting with solutions to propose. When this happens, work will be required to concentrate on the process of problem solving. The best way to do this is to use a technique known as a rational-decision process.

A rational-decision process includes these steps:

1. Study, discuss, and analyze the situation.
2. Define the problem.
3. Set an objective.
4. State imperatives and desirables.
5. Generate alternatives.
6. Establish evaluation criteria.
7. Evaluate alternatives.
8. Choose among alternatives.

When using this process, you first need to spend time discussing the situation and defining the problem. This ensures that you are dealing with the right problem. Then state an objective—the result you want to accomplish.

If imperatives exist, list them along with the desirable features of your eventual outcome; in other words, list both your needs and your wants. If there are mutually exclusive imperatives, they must be reconciled or you cannot solve the problem. Obviously, you want as few imperatives as possible.

Next, generate alternatives, through whatever method you choose. Then, set up some evaluation criteria, evaluate the alternatives against those criteria, and make a decision. You will have come to your decision with a straightforward, orderly process.

Generating Alternatives

Alternatives can generated in several ways. The most common is by open discussion. Two procedures will likely produce more alternatives and reflect greater creativity: brainstorming and the nominal group technique.

Brainstorming is a freeform process that taps into the creative potential of a group through association. Power of association is a two-way current. When a group member voices an idea, this invites other ideas by stimulating the associative power of all other members.

The *nominal group technique* has group members write down individual ideas and then report them to the group. It minimizes conformity while maximizing participation.

When choosing between these techniques, consider whether participants have enough experience to deal with the information you seek. If they know the information, the nominal group technique gives you an orderly method for getting it reported to the group. If participants do not know the information, brainstorming will create potential alternatives.

Brainstorming Procedures

- List all ideas offered by group members.
- Do not evaluate or judge ideas at this time.
- Do not discuss ideas except perhaps briefly to clarify understanding.
- Welcome "blue sky" ideas. It is always easier to eliminate than to accumulate.
- Allow repetition. Do not waste time sorting out duplication.
- Encourage quantity. The more ideas, the better.
- Avoid being eager to close out this phase. When a plateau is reached, let things rest and then start again.

Nominal Group Technique Procedures

- Each member writes ideas in response to a question presented to the group.
- Group members take turns reporting what they have written, one idea at a time. List the ideas in front of the group.
- Members add new ideas to the list after the group has finished reporting.
- The group continues the process until all ideas are listed.

Tip: ***When you are generating alternatives, you want ideas to flow freely. Do not allow evaluations and judgments during this time.***

Choosing Among Alternatives

After producing a number of alternatives, group members need to decide which alternatives they will choose to study further or implement. Several decision-making procedures are available. These tend to be either individual-centered or group-centered. Individual-centered procedures are consolidations of individual choices, while group-centered procedures rely on discussion and agreement.

The decision-making methods most commonly used are voting, consensus, and the nominal group technique.

Voting

This form of decision making is appropriate in larger groups. It should be used in small groups only as a backup style or when the decision being made is not critical. You can decide based on simple majority, or to reduce resistance to the final decision, you can set a higher number of votes needed to make the decision, such as 60% of the votes.

Consensus

This form of decision making maximizes the support of the decision by participants. By nature, it is a highly interactive process and tends to produce good decisions with a high level of commitment. The consensus process uses available resources to creatively resolve conflicts.

Consensus is sometimes difficult to reach, so not every group decision can be made in this way. Consensus is not the same as complete unanimity. However, each individual should be able to accept the group's decision. When all group members feel this way, you have reached a consensus and can state the group's decision.

Following are some guidelines for achieving consensus:

- Avoid arguing for your position. Present your position as lucidly and logically as possible, but listen to the other members' reactions and consider them carefully.
- Do not assume that someone must win and someone must lose when discussions reach a stalemate. Instead, look for the next-most acceptable alternative for all parties.
- Do not change your mind simply to avoid conflict. When agreement seems to come too quickly and easily, think further. Explore the reasons for the agreement, and be sure everyone accepts the solution for basically similar or complementary reasons. Yield only to positions that have objective and logically sound foundations.

- Avoid conflict-reducing techniques such as voting, averaging, and bargaining. When a dissenting member finally agrees, do not feel that person must be rewarded by being allowed to "win" on some later point.
- Differences of opinion are natural and expected. Seek them out and try to involve everyone in the decision-making process. Disagreements can help the group's decision; with a wide range of information and opinions, there is a greater chance that the group will hit upon a better solution.

The Nominal Group Technique

This form of decision making minimizes conformity and moves participants toward decisions they can support. As in the nominal group procedure for generating ideas, this process starts with the participants putting their choices in writing. Here are the steps involved:

1. After discussing the alternatives, individuals independently rate each alternative on a numerical scale, against an agreed-upon criterion such as time or cost.
2. Members report their ratings for each alternative, and the ratings are then added together.
3. If a clear choice appears, the process is complete. If not, alternatives with low total ratings are dropped from the list.
4. Members again discuss and rate the remaining alternatives independently. Again, if no clear choice appears, the alternatives with the lowest ratings are dropped from the list.
5. This process is repeated as required until a clear group choice remains.

Criteria-Based Decisions

Whatever decision-making process the group uses, setting criteria for choices is an important step. The criteria should be concepts that are important in the implementation of the ideas. You might have already them chosen before the meeting starts. For example, project completion time might be a priority, or the solution must work for several departments. Sometimes these concerns come up as part of the discussion, or the group leader may ask members to set these criteria just before the group begins the decision-making process.

Criteria-Based Rating

Evaluations can be on a subjective scale such as High, Moderate, Low, or on a scale such as 1 to 5 or 1 to 10; or actual values can be used, such as price, weight, or delivery time.

After agreeing on appropriate criteria such as feasibility, availability, and affordability, the group rates each alternative on either a numerical scale or a low, moderate, high scale. You can accomplish this rating by discussion or by consolidating individual ratings. Here is an example.

Sample Criteria-Based Rating Worksheet

List appropriate criteria across the top. (Usually one to four will be sufficient.) The final choice will be the alternative that rates the best on the most criteria. In this example, the group has used high, moderate, and low ratings.

	Criteria		
Alternatives	1. Time	2. Cost	3. Possible Start Date
1. *Buy new software*	*Low*	*High*	*Low (soon)*
2. *Create new software*	*High*	*Moderate*	*High*
3. *Change procedures*	*Moderate*	*Unknown*	*High*
4.			
5.			
6.			
7.			
8.			
9.			
10.			

Criteria-Based Ranking

In criteria-based ranking, members rank each alternative for a single criterion. After all the alternatives are ranked, members base their final choice on the one that ranks highest overall.

Sample Criteria-Based Ranking Worksheet

List participants' individual rankings (for participants A, B, C, and so forth), and then add across to get a total of individual rankings. The lowest total reflects the highest consolidated ranking. In this example, participants believe that buying new software is the least costly alternative.

Criterion: Cost

	Participants' Rankings						
Alternatives	**A**	**B**	**C**	**D**	**E**	**F**	**Total Ranking**
1. *Buy new software*	5	4	2	1	3	5	20
2. *Create new software*	4	2	1	3	3	2	15
3. *Change procedures*	2	1	5	3	2	3	15
4.							
5							
6							
7.							
8.							
9.							
10.							

Criteria-Based Paired Comparison

In this method, you list each alternative twice—on a horizontal line and on the corresponding vertical line. Compare alternative 1 to alternative 2. If 1 rates higher, put an "X" in the box; if 2 rates higher, leave the box blank. Continue across, comparing 1 to all the other alternatives; then go to the next line and repeat the process until all pairs have been compared.

Count the "X's" across for each alternative, and enter the number in the far right column. Then transfer the totals to the line labeled "number of X's" at the bottom of the chart. Count the blanks down and enter the total in the appropriate line at the bottom. Add the number of "X's" and blanks for each alternative, and enter results in the line marked "Total." The largest total will be the number-1 choice, next highest, number 2, etc. In a tie occurs, go back and compare the two again.

		Alternatives										
	Yes = X No = Blank	1.	2.	3.	4.	5.	6.	7.	8.	9.	10.	Number of X's
Alternatives	1.											
	2.											
	3.											
	4.											
	5.											
	6.											
	7.											
	8.											
	9.											
	10.											
	Number of Blanks											
	Number of X's:											
	TOTAL											
	Priority											

From: *Management by Objectives and Results for Business and Industry,* by George L. Morrisey (Addison-Wesley Publishing Co., 1977). Used by permission of the author.

Part Summary

In this part, you learned about the role of the meeting leader and the major components of a meeting. You learned how to structure both information meetings and decision-making meetings. Finally, you learned how to use the criteria-based rating, criteria-based ranking, and criteria-based paired comparison methods to help participants of a decision-making meeting evaluate options.

P A R T **4**

Leading Effective Discussions

"A sense of humor is part of the art of leadership, of getting along with people, of getting things done."

–Dwight D. Eisenhower

In this part:

- Stimulating Discussion
- Twenty Tips for Generating Discussion
- Handling Difficult Situations
- Understanding Conflict

Stimulating Discussion

Whether meeting participants are generating alternatives, considering pros and cons, or making choices, the success of any discussion depends on participation. When participants see that a mutual sharing of opinions and ideas is welcome, there is an atmosphere of free exchange. The leader's skillful use of questions will encourage productive discussions.

As a leader, you need to pay close attention to what is happening in the group. Notice if some members seem to be inactive. Pay attention to the pace of the discussion. Watch for cues from the group that suggest problems. If participants begin to fidget, look bored, or show by their expressions that they do not understand or they disagree, you should ask questions to find out what is going on and keep the discussion flowing.

Four types of questions are helpful in stimulating discussions:

- General questions, which elicit a broad range of potential responses
- Specific questions, which focus on a single idea, leaving a limited range of responses
- Overhead questions, which you ask the whole group, allowing volunteers to respond
- Direct questions, which you ask a selected individual

General and *overhead* questions are less threatening and are therefore better for starting a discussion. *Direct* and *specific* questions are best used after participants become comfortable with group discussion.

Things to Avoid

The following are likely to detract from discussions:

- **Unanswerable questions** — Be sure that the questions you ask can be answered by the group or by some member of the group.
- **Questions of simple assent or dissent** — Unless followed by other questions, like why, when, where, how, what, or who, questions with a yes or no answer lead nowhere.
- **Vague, ambiguous questions** — To get satisfactory answers, you must ask clear questions. Sometimes you may need to rephrase a question or break it down into sub-questions if it is not immediately understood. Never try to play with words or trap a participant into an incorrect or misleading answer.
- **Forceful words** — You may have to ask questions in the interest of clarification, but remember that you are not out to prove anything. Your approach should never be one that makes the person answering feel threatened.

"Jenkins is handing out brain hats to stimulate our thinking."

THINK ABOUT IT

In meetings you've recently attended, how has the leader's questioning style contributed to the level of discussion?

In recent meetings, what "things to avoid" have you observed? What effect have these questions had on the discussion?

What types of questions are most often used in the meetings you attend?

Twenty Tips for Generating Discussion

The following examples of questions and statements provide some useful guidelines for generating discussions.

1. **Ask for feelings and opinions.**

   What is your reaction to…?

   How do you feel about…?

   What is your thinking on…?

   What brings you to that conclusion?

2. **Paraphrase.**

   Let me see if I understand your position. Are you saying that…?

   Let me restate your last point to see if I understand.

   Before you go on, do you mean that…?

   Are you asking me to…?

3. **Encourage participation.**

   Lee, what do you think about this?

   Austin, how would you answer Sherri's questions?

   We have heard from everyone but Jane. Jane, what do you think?

   Dave, you had your say. Now it's Bob's turn. Give him a chance to explain.

4. **Ask for a summary.**

   We have several proposals. Can someone summarize what we've agreed to?

   It is clear that Jim doesn't agree. Jim, can you summarize your objections?

   We seem to be off track. Will someone summarize what has been done so far?

5. **Ask for clarification.**

   I didn't understand that last comment. What did you mean when you said you could…?

   The examples you gave concern weekday tasks. What about weekends?

   Jane's shaking her head. Jane, what can we do to help you with this issue?

   It is still not clear to me. What did you say we usually do when…?

6. **Ask for examples.**

   Dana, will you give some examples of what you mean?

   José, can you expand on that? I'm not sure I understand.

7. **Initiate action.**

   How do you think we should…?

   Frank, how would you suggest we proceed on this?

   I'd like some suggestions on how to get started. Jo, what do you propose?

8. **Explore an idea in more detail.**

   What are some other ways to approach this problem?

   Are there other things we should consider?

   Robin, what would you add to what has been said?

9. **Do a quick survey.**

   Let's see a show of hands. How many are for this proposal?

   Kira, why don't you ask the others what they think about your proposal?

   How does everybody feel about this? Let's start with Luis.

   Let's all take a couple of minutes to jot down a reaction to this proposal.

10. **Suggest a break.**

    We have been working on this for quite a while. How about a quick stand-and-stretch break?

    We have been working for about and hour and a half. How about a 10-minute break?

11. **Suggest a procedure.**

    Would it help if we list the agenda items in order of importance before we start?

    Let's stop the discussion for a few minutes. I think it might help if we each told the group what we're feeling right now.

    Let's go around the table so everyone has a chance to comment.

12. **Share your feelings.**

    I'm feeling a little irritated; you are not giving Kerry a chance to explain his position.

    I'm frustrated. I think we should take up this problem next week when we have more facts. What do the rest of you think?

13. **Reflect what you think someone else is feeling or thinking.**

    I get the impression that you are not satisfied with my answer. Is that right?

    I think Kim's comments mean that he wants to ask some questions on this. Kim?

14. **Question assumptions.** (Don't use the word "assume.")

    Are you saying that unless we talk to their managers, they won't cooperate?

    Your suggestion implies that we cannot meet the schedule. Is that right?

    Your objection makes me think that we will not get promised deliveries. Can you explain that further?

15. **Check targets or direction.**

    Are we asking the right questions?

    Is this the best way to get their cooperation?

    Is this the only way to get it done?

16. **Confront differences.**

    Nick, you haven't said so, but I'm sensing you don't agree. Is that right?

    Casey, you seem to be holding back. Is there something you disagree with?

    Bridget, I'm not sure you understood what Willie was trying to say. Why don't you tell us what you heard him say before you state your objections?

17. **Reverse roles.**

    Why don't you take the role of a customer for a few minutes. Now, as a customer, how would you react to this proposal?

    If you were the district manager, how would you react to this proposal?

    How would you feel if these suggestions were made for our own department?

18. **Look ahead.**

    If we did it this way, what is the worst thing that could happen?

    If it doesn't work, what will we have lost?

    If it works, how will it affect next week's schedule?

19. **Test for consensus.**

    It seems that we have come to an agreement on this issue. Can I have a show of hands on this?

    Does everyone accept the idea that…?

    Before we go on to the next issue, let me check to make sure that all have agreed to….

20. **Focus on action.**

    We've considered every possibility. We must choose from three alternatives.

    We have discussed both sides carefully. It's time to make a choice.

Handling Difficult Situations

Because meetings depend on interaction, it is inevitable that problems will occur. Sometimes problems originate with people, sometimes they originate with procedures or logic (or lack thereof). In any case, it is the responsibility of the leader to activate discussion of the most profitable kind, to make sure participation is distributed among members of the group, and to keep the discussion headed in the right direction.

Problems with People

Good, balanced participation, with different points of view being shared, is essential for the success of your meetings. Here are some things that will help you handle various participation problems.

A Person Who Tends to Dominate the Discussion

A talkative participant must not be permitted to dominate the discussion. Sometimes a person may assume a dominant role because of being more experienced or more senior than others present. Often, if that is the case, others will sit back and give up the floor. When this happens, use direct questions to draw out other participants. It is helpful to avoid looking at the senior person when presenting a question, thus making it difficult for that person to get your attention.

If nothing else is effective, a private chat with the individual during a break may help.

A Person Who Wants to Argue

This individual may act like a "know-it-all" or a quibbler who takes delight in crossing up the leader. Usually, such a person irritates the group, inviting unfavorable reactions. In any case, you as leader must remain calm. You can try using clarifying questions, which push the person to think about what he or she is saying. Then use direct questions to other participants as a means of maintaining the balance.

Often an argumentative person will recognize what has happened and will not present further problems. However, if the person is insensitive, you might have to be very direct, pointing out that the quibbling is interrupting the progress of the meeting and is wasting valuable time. You should then immediately turn to another person with a question to take the discussion forward.

A Person Who Starts Another Meeting with Neighbors

This problem is more likely to occur in a larger group. It may be the result of a talkative individual's need to speak when unable to address the group as a whole, or it may be the result of a more cautious thinker's desire to try out an idea before bringing it up to the entire group. Side conversations are inevitable in a typical meeting and are apt to be brief. They become a problem only if they are prolonged.

One technique is to invite the individual to share with everyone what is being said. Another way to handle this situation is to simply be quiet and look at the offending person. Typically, this will bring the meeting back to order.

A Person Who Is Timid or Lacking in Self-Confidence

Whether such a person feels uncertain because of inexperience or is simply unwilling to speak due to fear of embarrassment, you should ask a question in an area where the reluctant individual can speak with conviction. Usually, once the ice has been broken and anxiety dissolved, the individual will become a thoughtful contributor.

A Person Who Is Antagonistic or Skeptical

Sometimes people are antagonistic to the meeting or the leader, or are skeptical about the use of time. Usually such attitudes come from previous experiences with meetings or unskilled leaders. Give these people time. Once your meeting is under way and working well, they may see the difference and begin to participate.

A Person Who Attempts to Get an Opinion Instead of Give One

Experience has taught some people that not all managers or meeting leaders are open to new ideas, and some tend to force their own views on the group. In this case, participants may reply to questions with another question. In this situation, the best technique is to refer the question back to the group and then back to the person who asked it.

Problems with Procedures

The following situations are impersonal. They call for a different kind of response.

Establishing and Holding the Interest of the Group

It is essential to activate the group's attention in the opening statement and then motivate people to respond. Use visual aids as the discussion progresses. Case studies for group analysis are also effective. If responses lag, change the approach. Keep things moving.

Your voice can be an effective tool to help spark interest. If interest is waning, speak more loudly, more rapidly, and with more feeling. Typically this will pick up the energy of the meeting.

Handling Touchy Subjects

Anticipate what touchy subjects might arise and face them squarely. If they are not truly pertinent to the subject under discussion, point that out, referring to the objectives of the meeting. If they are pertinent, remain neutral, insisting on an objective consideration of the question. Do not promise to get action from management; promise only to report the conclusions or findings.

Developing Discussion and Avoiding Superficiality

Be prepared to cite specific cases and facts for consideration, if they are not forthcoming from group members. Call on individuals known to have specific relevant experiences. Encourage members to take issue with trends and to avoid the "bandwagon." Encourage original thought. Probe opinions for factual or conceptual bases. Do not permit oversimplification of anything.

Think About It

In meetings you've recently attended, what difficult situations have you observed involving problems with people? How did the meeting leader deal with these situations?

In those meetings, what difficult situations have you observed involving problems with procedures? How did the meeting leader deal with these situations?

How Would You Handle These Situations?

Rank your choices for these situations. Place a 1 in the blank for the answer you favor most, 2 in the blank of your next choice, and follow with a 3 and a 4.

1. Some participants are not contributing, although they appear to be attentive.

    ____ a. Monitor the situation to see if it continues.

    ____ b. Ask a noncontributing participant for an opinion or reaction.

    ____ c. Ask the participants why they are not more involved.

    ____ d. Do nothing. They'll speak up if they have something to say.

2. You want discussion on a topic, but no one is talking.

    ____ a. Ask a general question of the group.

    ____ b. Ask a specific question of an individual.

    ____ c. Ask for feedback on why no one is talking.

    ____ d. Adjourn the meeting due to lack of interest.

3. You notice, through nonverbal cues, that the group's interest level is fading.

    ____ a. Shorten your agenda and adjourn the meeting.

    ____ b. Take a five-minute break.

    ____ c. Speak more loudly and in a more animated fashion.

    ____ d. Try to start a discussion.

4. You get a question you cannot answer.

    ____ a. Redirect the question to the group.

    ____ b. Ignore the question.

    ____ c. Ask the person who asked the question the reason for it.

    ____ d. Admit that you do not know the answer, and move on.

CONTINUED

CONTINUED

5. A participant is spending too much time on an item that's not on the agenda.

____ a. Interrupt and point out the need to get back to the agenda.

____ b. Do nothing and hope the meeting makes some progress.

____ c. Ask participants if they want to discuss the subject.

____ d. Tell the participant that the topic will be taken up at the end of the meeting if there is enough time.

6. The group is getting away from the objective of the meeting.

____ a. Let things go as long as everyone seems interested.

____ b. Interrupt and bring the group back to the agenda.

____ c. Interrupt and vote on whether to continue this discussion.

____ d. Take a break so participants can continue the discussion on their own time; then reconvene when it is over.

7. Two people, sitting together, keep whispering to each other. It has been going on for some time. You find it distracting.

____ a. Ask them to share their discussion with the group.

____ b. Ask them a content-related question to see if they're listening.

____ c. Stop talking and look at them.

____ d. Ignore it and hope they finish soon.

8. A participant's comments seem intended to embarrass you, the leader.

____ a. Ask the person for clarification.

____ b. Ask direct questions of other meeting participants.

____ c. Do nothing and hope the individual gets on board.

____ d. Confront the individual about disrupting the meeting.

Compare your answers with the author's suggested responses in the Appendix.

Understanding Conflict

Interpersonal conflict in meetings is not necessarily bad. In fact, it can be healthy when handled properly. Therefore, the question is not how to eliminate conflict, but how to capitalize on its constructive aspects. In many instances, interpersonal differences, competition, rivalry, and other forms of conflict contribute to the effectiveness of the meeting.

A moderate level of conflict might have these constructive consequences:

- Increased motivation and energy to do a task
- Increased innovative thinking, through a greater diversity of viewpoints
- Increased understanding of a position on an issue, by forcing the advocate of that position to articulate it and support it with facts
- Increased understanding of opposing positions on an issue, by forcing participants to listen and then to integrate diverse positions to achieve consensus

When all participants are doing their best, conflict is natural. What is best for one department, for example, won't necessarily be the best for others. Conflict management is a primary skill for conducting effective meetings.

What Causes Conflict?

Conflict occurs when the desires of two individuals or groups appear incompatible. It often occurs when individuals come to a meeting with preconceived ideas about the outcome, rather than planning to work together to find a solution that is acceptable to the group. Here are four classic conditions that often lead to conflict:

- **Miscommunication** — People often don't listen well. As a result, misunderstandings occur that may lead to conflict.
- **Different perceptions** — Two or more people experience a common event but come away with different views of what happened.
- **Different values** — Different value systems lead people to define acceptable actions differently.
- **Different preferred outcomes** — Two or more people want different solutions to the same problem.

Managing Conflict

How conflict is handled will have a dramatic impact on the group and its members' ability to work together. There are two dynamics to be sensitive to:

- The concern people have for winning a point
- The concern for maintaining relationships

Five Approaches

How these two dynamics interrelate determines which of five approaches you'll want to use to deal with a conflict: demanding, problem solving, bargaining, giving in, or delaying. Each approach is appropriate under the right circumstances. Frequently, however, people do not analyze conflict and so do not choose an appropriate approach. The tendency is to use a comfortable strategy in all situations, but this often leads to addressing conflict improperly, and it can damage important relationships.

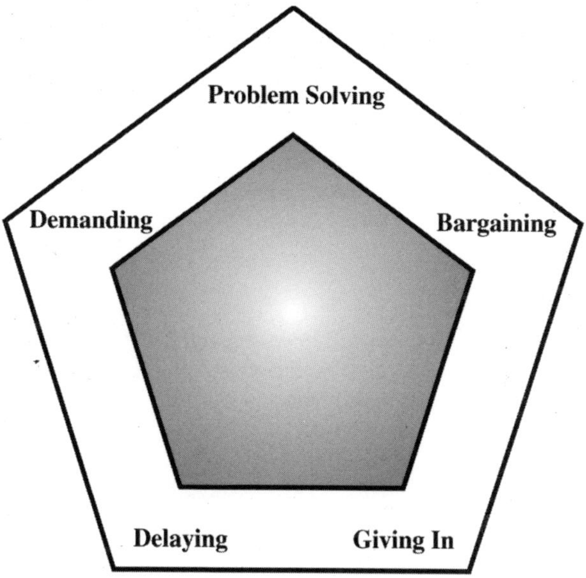

Demanding

This approach suggests that winning is more important than the relationship. Demanding is a form of aggressiveness and often evokes an aggressive response. While it maximizes an individual's outcome, it is usually at the expense of the relationship because, in demanding, there is a winner and a loser. Most people do not like to lose.

Problem Solving

This approach shows high concern for both winning and maintaining the relationship. Both parties work together actively to find a mutually satisfactory solution to a common problem. In a meeting, it requires joint problem solving, which in turn leads to creative solutions and a commitment to carry them out.

Bargaining

Bargaining is a backup position when neither demanding nor problem solving leads to a solution. Bargaining remains moderately high on both concerns, winning and maintaining the relationship. It is most effective when both parties are willing to give a little to resolve their differences.

Giving In

With this response, maintaining the relationship is viewed as more important than winning the point. It is also an appropriate response when new information invalidates a position. In meetings you conduct, you may need to help participants find face-saving ways to give up their positions on issues under discussion.

Delaying

Not every conflict needs to be resolved immediately. Delaying confrontation can be appropriate when the issue is trivial. You can also delay temporarily to give people time to cool off or to gather additional facts.

Tips for Moving Through Conflict

There are specific things you can do to help a group move through conflict. The following ideas should help you handle this in a positive way.

Clarify Objectives

Conflicts sometimes develop because participants have different understandings of the meeting's objectives. Clarifying and reaching agreement on objectives is an important first step.

Strive for Understanding

Often, when involved in argument, people do not listen carefully to the opposition. They are too busy formulating a rebuttal. As the meeting leader, you may find it necessary to stop the action and make sure each party in a conflict can state the opposing party's position and supporting reasons.

Focus on the Rational

Emotional involvement is a natural part of confrontation. But sound decisions cannot be reached when participants are too emotional. For the benefit of the outcome, keep attention focused on rational considerations, such as facts, supporting reasons, and potential problems if a certain course of action is followed.

Generate Alternatives

What alternate solutions integrate the needs of the diverse points of view involved in the confrontation? This is a challenging part of the process, because participants often cannot see any alternative to their solutions. This is where group members who are not at either extreme can become a resource to generate some reasonable alternatives.

Table the Issue

Tabling can be an effective way to deal with conflict when you think that a party needs time to consider the arguments that have been presented. It works particularly well as a face-saving device. People sometimes find themselves in a position of having argued so strongly for a position that they cannot gracefully change even after being convinced of the logic of a different position. Tabling gives a person time to work this out.

Use Humor

If you are good with humor, you can use it to reduce the tension of confrontation. Humor can serve as a release and clear the way for more rational problem solving.

Other Ways to Handle Conflict in Meetings

Other approaches that can help you handle conflict in meetings include:

- Acknowledging deadlines
- Involving everyone in the process
- Allowing time to think
- Taking a break (i.e., calling a time-out)
- Referring items to a subcommittee
- Allowing the expression of strong feelings
- Protecting the group from early closure

Handling Conflict Between Two Groups

When two groups disagree about how to resolve a problem, you can stop the discussion and deal with the conflict in the following way. Ask each group member to indicate where he or she stands on the following scale:

For 5 4 3 2 1 0 1 2 3 4 5 **Against**

When group members have indicated their positions, ask them to post their scores on a flip chart. Then, ask group members who are *for* a given position to explain why other members are *against* the position. Do the same with the other group. Ask those who are against the position to explain why the others are for the position.

In this way, you can:

- Provide a quick way to get the issues surfaced.
- Get all pro and con ideas out in the open.
- Ensure that each group is listening and understands what the other group is saying and why.

Finally, invite those who are neutral on the issue to offer alternatives that can integrate the needs of those for and those against the issue under discussion.

Observation

Conflict should not be avoided in meetings. It is a natural outcome of strongly held points of view. But it is important to contain it and focus it toward resolution.

All conflict can be resolved. Not that it always will—but it can. Most often it is resolved through communication. One expert estimates that 70% of conflicts can be handled by simply using clear communication. Twenty percent will require negotiation. And the remaining 10% can be resolved through arbitration or the use of a third party.

Part Summary

In this part, you learned how to lead effective discussions. You learned how to stimulate discussions, what things to avoid in discussion, and how to generate more discussion. Next, you learned how to handle difficult situations with people and procedures. Then you learned how to understand and manage conflict in meetings.

P A R T **5**

Improving Meetings

"*Everything can be improved.*"

–C. H. Barron

In this part:

- An Improvement Model
- Evaluating Meetings
- Providing Feedback
- A Model for Effective Meetings
- Being a Productive Participant

An Improvement Model

Practice makes perfect only when you practice the right things. This section describes several tools you can use to improve the quality of meetings you attend, whether as a leader or as a participant.

The most important element in bringing about improvement is the motivation to improve. As a leader, you might have received feedback that your meetings lacked "something." Or you might have noticed that your meetings tend to drag on and accomplish little. As a participant, you might want to do more to contribute effectively to meetings you attend. Regardless of what brings you to realize that improvement is in order, nothing will change until you are motivated to make things happen.

The first step will be to single out the elements that need to be changed. This is where input from others is essential. The next few pages go into detail on how to have meetings evaluated. Once improvement areas have been identified, you need ideas on how best to handle those areas.

Finally, when you have developed a new set of actions, it is important to try them. Following each trial, evaluate the meeting to see if the change has been effective. If so, go on to the next area that needs improvement. If not, try something else until you solve the problem.

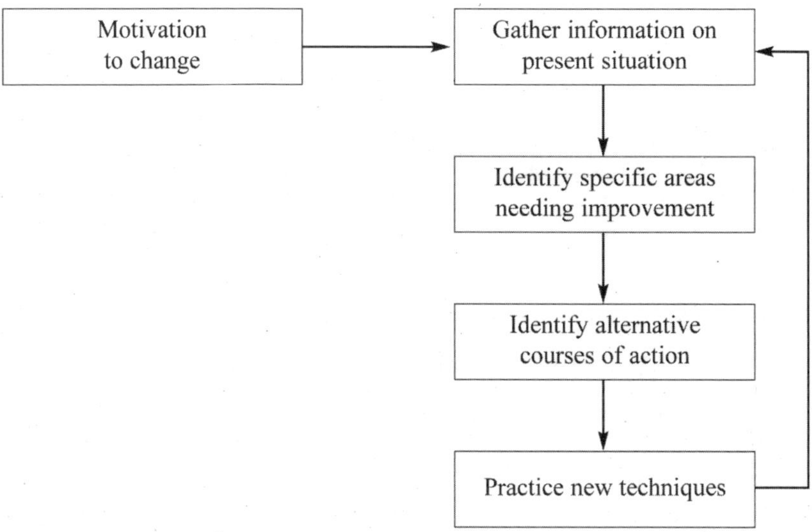

The improvement model

Evaluating Meetings

Effective meetings occur when leaders and participants work together to find a better way to get the job done. Participants come to a meeting with ideas, skills, knowledge, and experience. The leader's job is to create an environment where evaluation becomes a normal part of the process.

The benefits of an evaluation will be worthwhile if the following conditions exist:

- The leader wants to improve future meetings.
- The leader receives honest input from evaluators.
- Evaluators are candid in their assessments.
- The leader receives feedback in a positive way.
- The leader incorporates improvements into future meetings.

Sources of Evaluation

There are three potential sources for evaluating meetings:

- Self-evaluation by the leader
- Evaluation by a trained observer
- Evaluation by participants

All should contribute to improving a meeting. However, evaluations by trained observers and participants tend to be broader in scope and more objective.

Self-Evaluation by the Leader

After leading a meeting, you should ask yourself:

- How did I do?
- Where did things go well, and why?
- Where did I have problems, and why?
- What would I do differently next time?

This is the minimum evaluation to be considered. A leader will have impressions about things that went well and problem areas that were encountered. A few minutes reflecting on these experiences can be helpful.

Evaluation by a Trained Observer

A trained observer should be familiar with the ingredients of an effective meeting, skilled in making objective evaluations, and accomplished at giving feedback. It is difficult to find someone with all these qualifications.

A meeting observer typically sits in the back of the room and records notes on an evaluation form. Notes that follow a timeline of the meeting are most helpful. Following the meeting, the observer may either report to the group and invite discussion about how to improve the effectiveness of future meetings. Or the trained observer may choose to report privately to the meeting leader to discuss improvement needs.

Evaluation by Participants

Participants are an excellent resource for evaluation. They have feelings and reactions to meetings, events, and leadership styles that others may not choose to acknowledge. An open discussion is usually useful to get feedback from participants.

Timing of Evaluations

Evaluation can take place during the meeting, at the end of the meeting, or after the meeting has adjourned. Let's look at how you might use each of these times.

During the Meeting

This evaluation need not be formal or complicated. During any meeting, the leader can be alert for cues indicating that something needs improving. The cues can be verbal or nonverbal, subtle or blunt. The simplest (and most effective) way is to stop the meeting and deal directly with what is happening.

Another way to initiate an ongoing evaluation is to take time after a break and simply ask the group for comment:

- ▶ "How is the meeting going so far?"
- ▶ "What can we do to make our meeting more effective?"

Give participants time to think about the questions; then ask them to share their comments. Be prepared to listen carefully and respond to suggestions that are made.

At the End of the Meeting

If you have time at the end of the meeting, it might be worthwhile to ask everyone to complete a form and then post the scores on a flip chart for group discussion. The actual numbers are not of special importance. What is important is the opportunity to share perceptions of what is going on. The goal is to deal with items that can improve future meetings.

Use caution with end-of-meeting evaluations. Participants are often in a hurry, so they might not take the time to do a thorough evaluation. Be sure everyone has enough time to invest in the evaluation, or defer it until later.

After the Meeting

If you don't have time at the end of the meeting, or you want to give participants more time to evaluate the meeting, you can use these evaluation techniques:

- Distribute evaluation forms to participants as you adjourn; ask them to complete the forms and return them to you.
- Send evaluation forms to participants soon after the meeting; e-mail is often useful for this.
- Telephone a sampling of the group and request a narrative evaluation of the meeting.
- Visit with members of the meeting and ask them to evaluate it in a face-to-face discussion.

You will probably get better results if you set a deadline for the return of evaluation forms.

Meeting Evaluation Forms

The example on the next page illustrates the kind of form you can use to encourage people to examine their meetings. You may choose to develop your own evaluation form, using this one as a model.

When you use any evaluation form for a meeting, it is useful to keep it to one side of one page. Participants usually do not want to spend time, either at the end of a meeting or after the meeting, filling out more extensive forms.

MEETING EVALUATION WORKSHEET

1. Were the meeting's objectives clearly stated?

   Not At All 1 2 3 4 5 6 7 8 9 Completely

2. Did the meeting meet its stated objectives?

   Not At All 1 2 3 4 5 6 7 8 9 Completely

3. Did the meeting achieve your personal objectives?

   Not At All 1 2 3 4 5 6 7 8 9 Completely

4. Was the knowledge of participants used?

   Not At All 1 2 3 4 5 6 7 8 9 Completely

5. Was decision making shared by participants?

   Not At All 1 2 3 4 5 6 7 8 9 Completely

6. Did people trust and level with each other?

   Not At All 1 2 3 4 5 6 7 8 9 Completely

7. Were all participants actively involved in the meeting?

   Not At All 1 2 3 4 5 6 7 8 9 Completely

8. Did leadership style contribute to the meeting's effectiveness?

   Not At All 1 2 3 4 5 6 7 8 9 Completely

9. Which portions of the meeting were most helpful to you?

   ____

   ____

10. Which aspects were least helpful to you?

   ____

   ____

11. What action steps will you be taking as a result of this meeting?

   ____

   ____

12. Other comments?

   ____

   ____

Providing Feedback

Feedback allows people to receive information about their effect on others. It can help an individual keep his or her behavior on target and better achieve goals. Consider the following illustration.

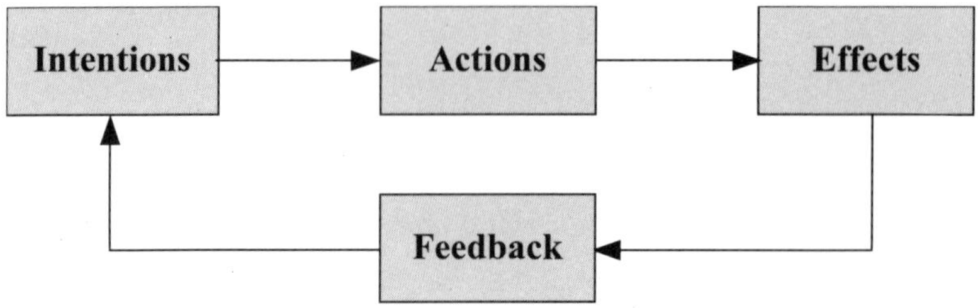

As the leader, it is appropriate for you to provide feedback. Feedback will usually be about an individual's behavior that either helped the meeting accomplish its purpose or was disruptive. It is important to provide positive feedback to participants when they do something that contributes to the meeting's effectiveness.

It is also important for you to be able to receive feedback that helps you improve your meeting skills, whether as leader or participant. When you receive feedback, ask questions that produce helpful, specific information.

Criteria for Useful Feedback

Following are criteria for providing feedback that is useful:

- Be descriptive rather than evaluative. By describing action, you leave the individual free to use or not use the information. By avoiding evaluative language, you reduce the chances of an individual reacting defensively.
- Be specific rather than general. To describe someone as "dominating" is not very useful. Instead, you can say something like, "I think you may be missing some valuable ideas in what others are saying."
- Direct feedback toward behavior that the receiver can do something about. Frustration is only increased when you remind people of shortcomings over which they have no control.
- Time it well. In general, feedback is most useful at the earliest opportunity after the behavior.
- Communicate feedback clearly. One way of ensuring this is to have the receiver rephrase the feedback to see if it corresponds to what you had in mind.

Examples of Feedback

Providing helpful, effective feedback is a skill that you can learn. The following examples can help you understand the differences between good and poor feedback.

Poor feedback	Better feedback
You are crude and disgusting.	Your suggestive stories make me uncomfortable.
You are rude and inconsiderate.	When you don't let me finish, I feel frustrated and think that you don't value my comments.
You're unfriendly.	I feel like I'm being left out.
You're a loudmouth.	I didn't get a chance to explain my position at the meeting.
You enjoy putting people down.	I think you didn't listen seriously to my point of view.
You don't care about anyone but yourself.	You seem unconcerned about me and what I can contribute.
You ran the meeting all wrong.	I'm disappointed that we couldn't reach a decision. What can we do better next time?
You are a wonderful person.	Thanks for backing me up.

"Let's wrap up with feedback on the training, and on Betty's mid-session freakout."

A Model for Effective Meetings

You can conduct more effective meetings by practicing the ideas presented in this book. This model for effective meetings reviews the most important points you've learned, putting them all together.

Before the Meeting

First, determine whether a meeting needs to be held. Avoid the trap of meeting too often. Be willing to cancel a meeting or adjourn early if there is nothing important to discuss. Deciding whether or not to meet depends on the objective you want to achieve. Once you establish an objective, you may find there is a better way to accomplish it than by holding a meeting.

If a meeting is appropriate, decisions must be made about when and where to meet and who should attend. When choosing a time, keep the needs of participants in mind. Avoid particularly busy times. The meeting site should be comfortable and free of distractions. It should comfortably accommodate the attendees. When choosing participants, be guided by who can either gain from attending or contribute by attending. Keep the number down to the minimum necessary to accomplish your purpose.

Next, develop an agenda and notify participants of the meeting. The agenda should list, in sequential order, items to be dealt with. It should also list the meeting's start time, any scheduled breaks, and a targeted ending time. A copy of the agenda should be sent to all participants in advance whenever possible. When this is not possible, an agenda should be developed as the first item of business.

During the Meeting

The day of the meeting, the leader should arrive at the meeting room early. During this time, it is important to check the room arrangement and change it if necessary. Also, check audiovisual equipment to ensure that it is operational.

Begin the meeting promptly at the scheduled time. An opening statement should include the meeting's objective, a brief review of the agenda, and any appropriate ground rules.

In an information meeting, present information in a clear, concise, easily understood style. Monitor the level of interest as reflected through nonverbal cues. Use varying voice levels to keep the energy level high. Change the format by asking questions if interest seems to lag. Get the group involved.

In a decision-making meeting, it is essential to facilitate the group's problem-solving and decision-making process. Monitor group interaction and suggest procedures to help make decisions. When there is too little interaction, generate discussion. When there is too much interaction, keep things focused and summarize the progress made so far. Techniques for displaying and analyzing data, generating alternatives, and choosing among alternatives will help you keep the group moving toward the objective.

Regardless of the type of meeting, close with a restatement of the objective, a summary of what was accomplished, and a list of agreed-upon actions that need to be taken.

After the Meeting

After the meeting, follow up on action points. A brief memorandum of conclusions should be written and distributed. Inform appropriate people who did not attend the meeting about essential decisions made.

Finally, each meeting should be viewed as a learning experience. Future meetings should be improved by soliciting evaluations and deciding what action steps are required to conduct better meetings.

Good luck! May all of your meetings be productive!

THINK ABOUT IT

Now that you have a model for effective meetings, in what ways do you need to improve your meeting leadership skills?

How do you plan to build evaluation and feedback into future meetings you lead?

RATE YOURSELF AS A MEETING LEADER

Check (√) yes (Y) or no (N) to each of the following questions based on how you act (or would act) as a meeting leader.

	Y	N
1. Do I have clear objectives for meetings?	❑	❑
2. Am I selective about the participants I invite?	❑	❑
3. Do I prepare agendas and distribute them in advance?	❑	❑
4. Do I arrive early enough to check arrangements?	❑	❑
5. Do I start meetings promptly regardless of who is present?	❑	❑
6. Do I follow an agenda?	❑	❑
7. Do I manage time and conclude on schedule?	❑	❑
8. Do I elicit everyone's participation?	❑	❑
9. Do I help in the resolution of conflict?	❑	❑
10. Do I maintain proper control of the discussion?	❑	❑
11. Do I summarize accomplishments at the end of meetings and clarify actions to be taken?	❑	❑
12. Do I prepare and distribute recaps of discussions?	❑	❑
13. Do I request evaluative feedback from participants?	❑	❑
14. Do I follow through on action items I've agreed to?	❑	❑
15. Do I follow up on action to be taken by others?	❑	❑

Being a Productive Participant

We have been focusing on leading meetings, but you can do a lot to make meetings effective by how you participate in the meetings you attend. Everyone is a meeting participant at one time or another. An effective meeting depends on productive participants. As a participant, you are in a position to make a significant contribution to the success of meetings you attend. All you need is a tactful way to ask questions and offer suggestions.

A productive participant demonstrates all of the behaviors previously mentioned for successful meetings. These include being on time, not carrying on side conversations, being willing to ask questions, paying attention, listening, and staying involved. Other helpful things you can do as a participant include:

- Staying focused on the meeting objectives and on the discussion
- Supporting useful ideas from the leader or other participants
- Judging the merit of ideas presented and not being distracted by delivery styles
- Delaying any judgment until the full idea has been presented
- Not allowing environmental conditions, such as noise or uncomfortable distractions, to distract you
- Taking well-organized notes

A good meeting participant:

- Prepares for the meeting
- Contributes ideas to the discussion
- Listens to the ideas of others
- Evaluates problems objectively
- Contributes to the orderly conduct of the meeting
- Provides feedback to the meeting leader
- Follows through on agreed-upon actions

RATE YOURSELF AS A MEETING PARTICIPANT

Check (√) yes (Y) or no (N) to each of the following questions based on how you act (or would act) as a meeting participant.

	Y	N
1. Do I typically know the purpose of the meetings I attend?	❑	❑
2. Do I understand my role in meetings I attend?	❑	❑
3. Do I confirm my attendance in advance?	❑	❑
4. Do I complete required "homework," such as looking up information or studying proposals?	❑	❑
5. Do I arrive before the scheduled start time?	❑	❑
6. Do I engage in side conversations while the meeting is in progress?	❑	❑
7. Do I leave meetings for reasons such as non-emergency phone calls?	❑	❑
8. Do I ask questions when I am not sure about something?	❑	❑
9. Am I typically open to the ideas of others?	❑	❑
10. Am I a good listener?	❑	❑
11. Do I actively participate in discussions when I have something worthwhile to contribute?	❑	❑
12. Do I help others stay on the subject?	❑	❑
13. After meetings, do I take the agreed-upon actions?	❑	❑
14. Do I contribute to improving meetings by giving feedback to those who conduct them, by a note, phone call, or visit?	❑	❑
15. After meetings, do I inform appropriate people who did not attend about what was discussed and the outcome?	❑	❑

Part Summary

In this part, you learned how to improve meetings. You learned how to evaluate meetings and provide useful feedback. Next, you learned about a model for effective meetings, which described what to do before, during, and after meetings. Finally, you learned how to be a productive participant in someone else's meeting.

APPENDIX

Appendix to Part 4

Comments & Suggested Responses

How Would You Handle These Situations?

1.
   a. 1
   b. 2
   c. 3
   d. 4

2.
   a. 1
   b. 2
   c. 3
   d. 4

3.
   a. 4
   b. 3
   c. 1
   d. 2

4.
   a. 1
   b. 4
   c. 2
   d. 3

5.
   a. 3
   b. 4
   c. 2
   d. 1

6.
   a. 3
   b. 1
   c. 2
   d. 4

7.
   a. 3
   b. 2
   c. 1
   d. 4

8.
   a. 2
   b. 1
   c. 4
   d. 3

Viva-Crisp 50-Minute
Titles in the Series

ISBN	Author	Title	YOP	Price
9788130918174	Gambino	**50 Minutes to Better Software Demos**: *Apply Your Sales Skills with Confidence*	2011	195.00
9788130918488	Bozek	**50 One-Minute Tips to Better Communications**: *Speak, Write and Present More Effectively, 3/e*	2011	250.00
9788130918211	Conlow & Watsabaugh	**Achieving Supervisory Excellence**: *Be the Leader Your People Need*	2011	195.00
9788130918396	McKnight & Chapman	**Attitude**: *Protect Your Most Priceless Asset, 5/e*	2011	245.00
9788130918495	Terry Dickey	**Basics of Budgeting**: *Become a Better Business Planner, 2/e*	2011	250.00
9788130918310	Conlow & Watsabaugh	**Become a Successful Supervisor**: *Develop Essential People Skills*	2011	225.00
9788130918327	Brock	**Better Business Writing**: *Become A More Powerful Communicator, 5/e*	2011	225.00
9788130918228	Dupont	**Business Etiquette & Professionalism**: *Conduct Yourself With Confidence, 3/e*	2011	195.00
9788130918181	Morgan	**Calming Upset Customers**: *Stay in Control ... In any Situation, 4/e*	2011	195.00
9788130918198	Minor	**Coaching and Counseling**: *Become a Better Manager Through Mentoring, 4/e*	2011	195.00
9788130918273	Decker	**Communication Skills for Leaders**: *Deliver a Clear and Consistent Message, 4/e*	2011	225.00
9788130918143	Kindler	**Conflict Management**: *Resolve Disagreement at Work, 4/e*	2011	165.00
9788130918280	Conlow & Watsabaugh	**Creating a High Performance Team**: *Gain the Skills of Today's Successful Leaders*	2011	225.00
9788130918334	Feldman	**Critical Thinking**: *Make Strategic Decisions With Confidence, 2/e*	2011	225.00
9788130918426	Flynn	**E-Mail Management**: *Keep Your Inbox Under Control, 2/e*	2011	245.00
9788130918471	Kravitz & Schubert	**Emotional Intelligence Works**: *Think, Be and Work Smarter, 3/e*	2011	245.00
9788130918150	Maddux	**Ethics in Business**: *Manage With Authority and Fairness, 2/e*	2011	195.00
9788130918235	Rouillard	**Goals and Goal Setting**: *Achieve Measurable Results, 4/e*	2011	195.00
9788130918204	Conlow Watsabaugh	**Handling Difficult People and Situations**: *Lead People Through Adversity*	2011	195.00

	Author	Title	YOP	Price
3433	Wendover	**High Performance Hiring**: *Select the Best Every Time, 3/e*	2011	245.00
9788130918402	Shea	**Making the Most of Being Mentored**: *Mentors Help Mentees Do, 2/e*	2011	245.00
9788130918242	Scott	**Managing Personal Change**: *Stay Positive and Stay in Control, 3/e*	2011	195.00
9788130918341	Haynes	**Meeting Skills for Leaders**: *Make Meetings More Productive, 4/e*	2011	225.00
9788130918440	Shea	**Mentoring**: *Make It A Mutually Rewarding Experience, 4/e*	2011	245.00
9788130918525	Shandler	**Motivating the Millennial Knowledge Worker**: *Help Today's Workforce Succeed in Today's Economy*	2011	395.00
9788130918167	Mandel	**Presentation Skills**: *Captivate and Educate Your Audience, 4/e*	2011	195.00
9788130918518	Pokras	**Problem Solving for Teams**: *Make Consensus More Achievable, 3/e*	2011	295.00
9788130918259	Haynes	**Project Management**: *Get from the Idea to Implementation Successfully, 4/e*	2011	195.00
9788130918372	Martin	**Quality Customer Service**: *Satisfy Customers– It's Everybody's Job, 5/e*	2011	245.00
9788130918457	Lightle & Doucet	**Sexual Harassment in the Workplace**: *Create a Better Workplace For Everyone, 3/e*	2011	245.00
9788130918501	Lengefeld	**Study Skills Strategies**: *Get the Most From Every Minute of Learning, 4/e*	2011	250.00
9788130918358	Conlow & Watsabaugh	**SuperSTAR Customer Service**: *It's all about C.A.R.E.*	2011	225.00
9788130918297	Maddux & Wingfield	**Team Building**: *Turn Personal Strengths Into Group Success, 5/e*	2011	225.00
9788130918464	Finch	**Telephone Courtesy & Customer Service**: *Be Your Company's Lifeline to Customers, 4/e*	2011	245.00
9788130918389	Conlow & Watsabaugh	**Telephone Skills that Satisfy Customers**: *Unleash the Full Potential of the Telephone*	2011	245.00
9788130918303	Romero	**The Business of Listening**: *Become a More Effective Listener, 4/e*	2011	225.00
9788130918365	Chapman & McKnight	**The New Supervisor**: *Lead With Confidence, 5/e*	2011	225.00
9788130918266	Haynes	**Time Management**: *Get An Extra Day a Week*	2011	195.00
9788130918419	Gill & Chatton	**Understanding Financial Statements**: *Master the Tools That Help You Succeed, 3/e*	2011	245.00